AF587295

Daniel Lergon

UNTER GRÜN

HATJE
CANTZ

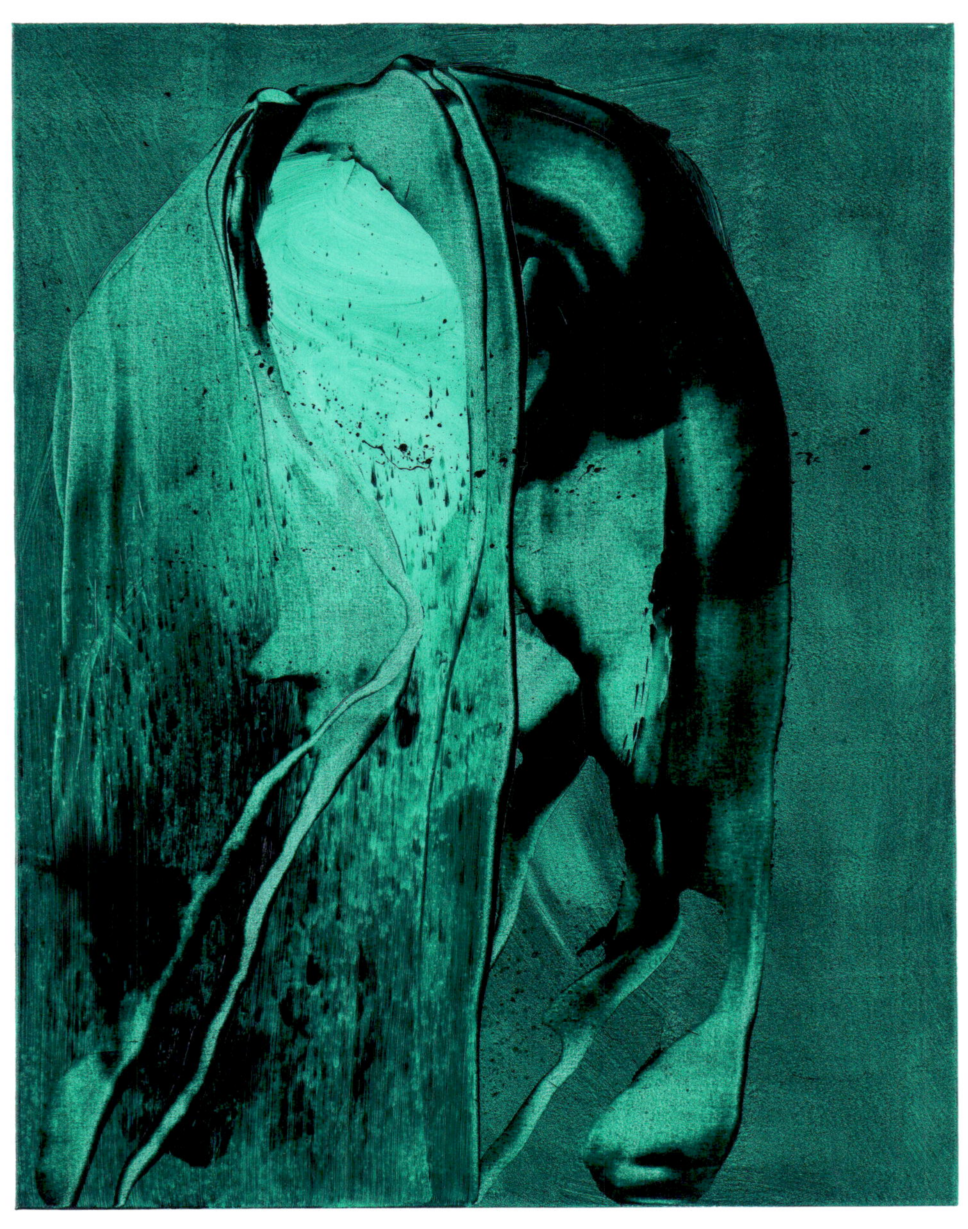

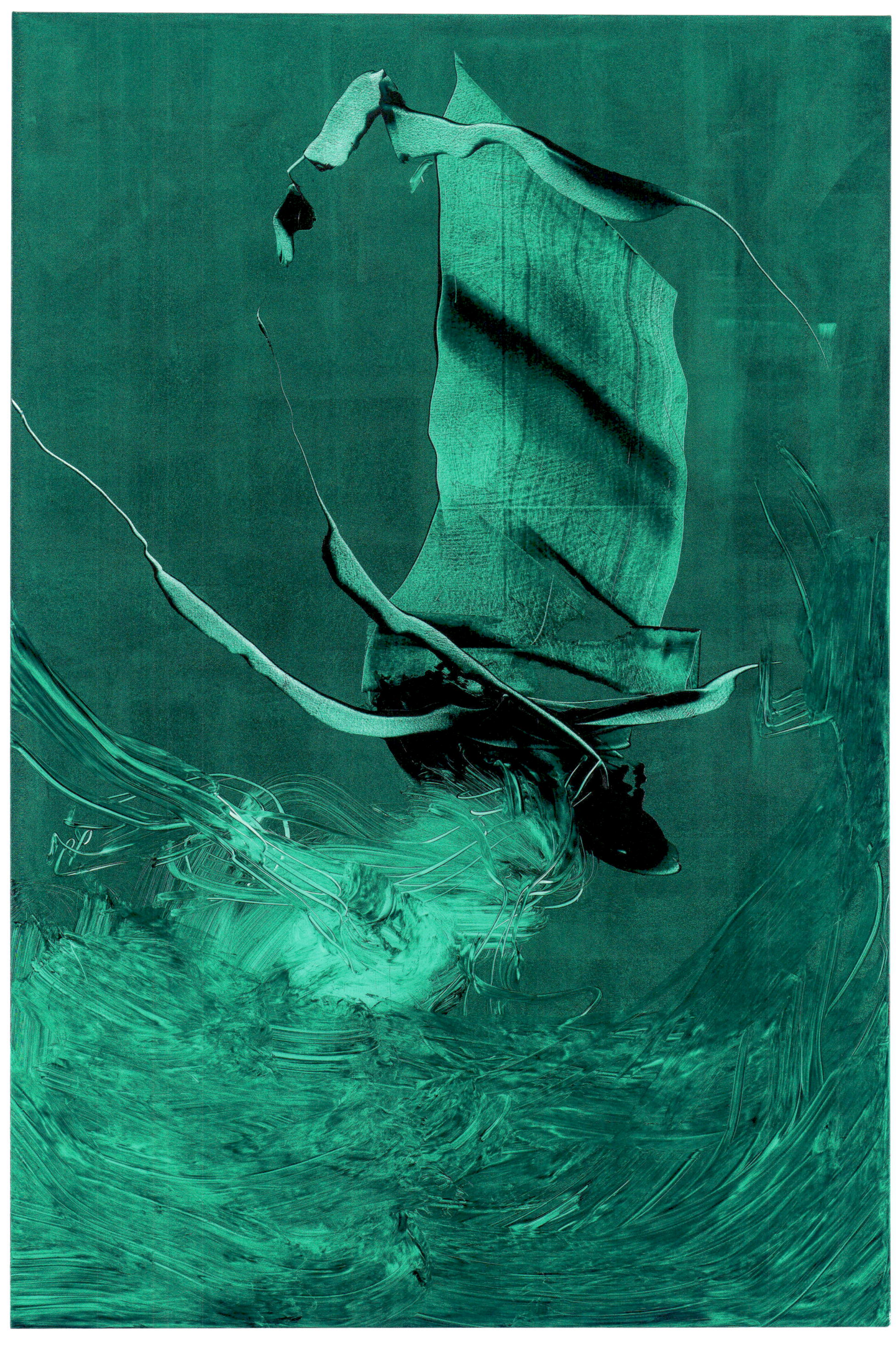

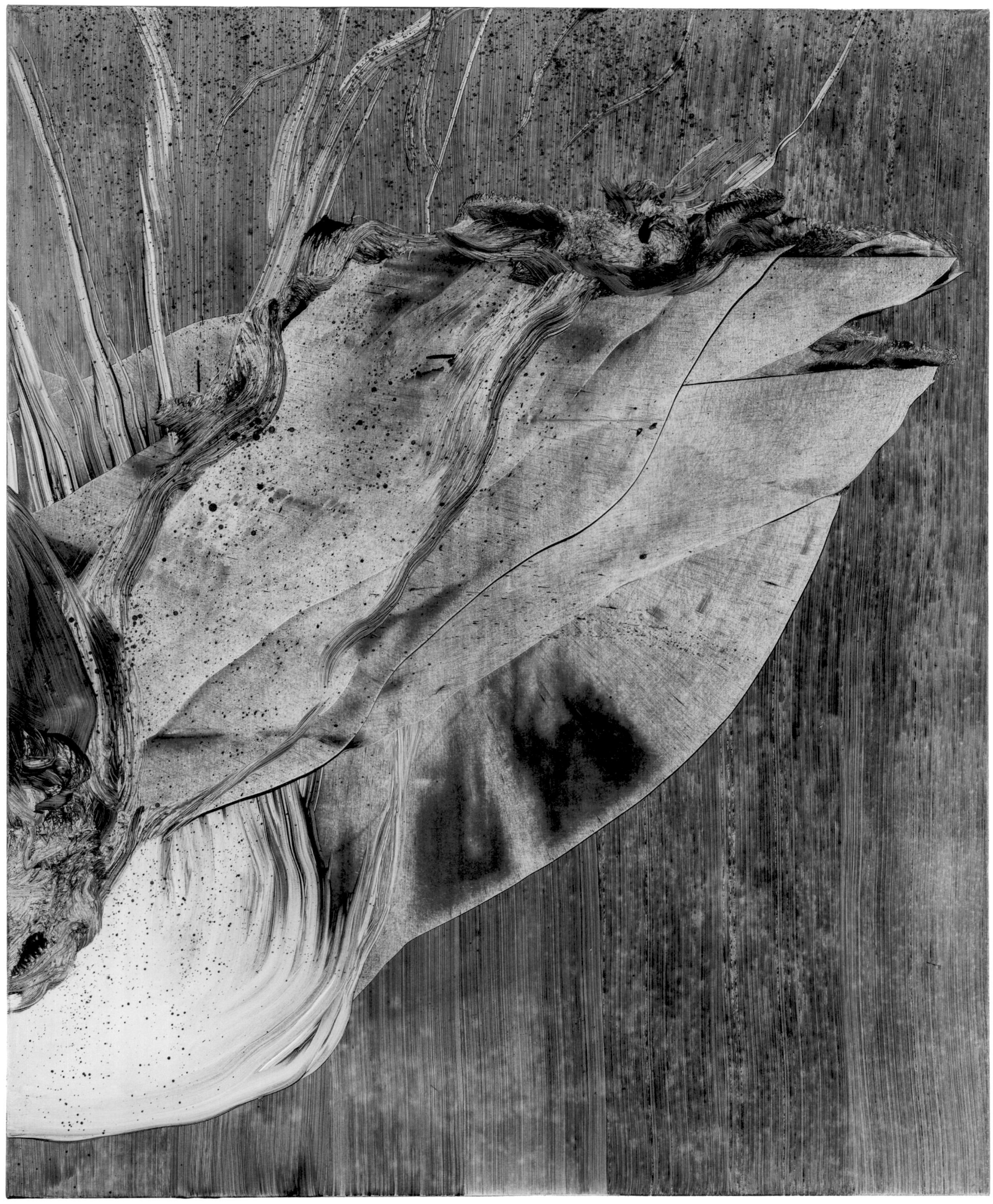

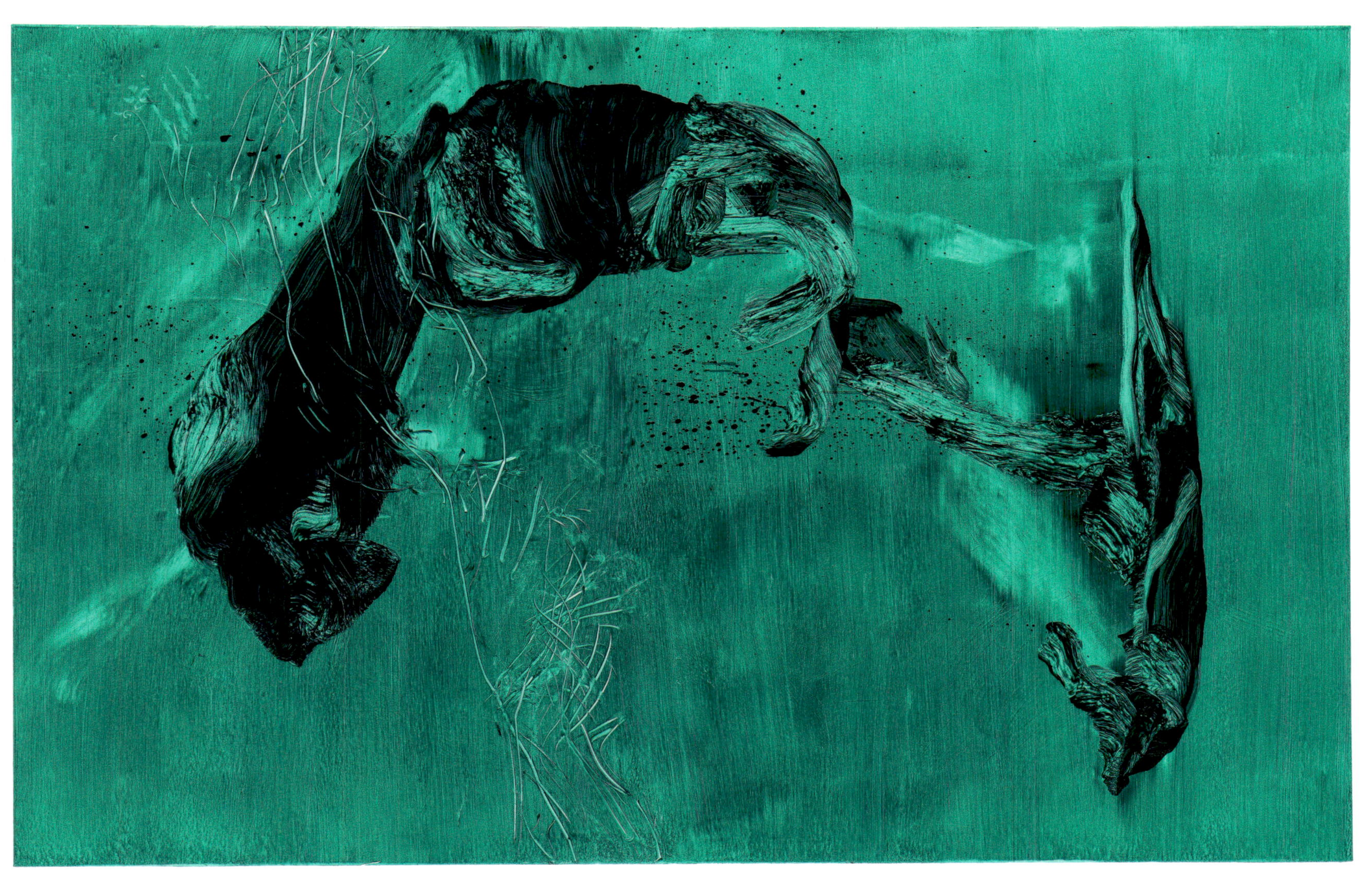

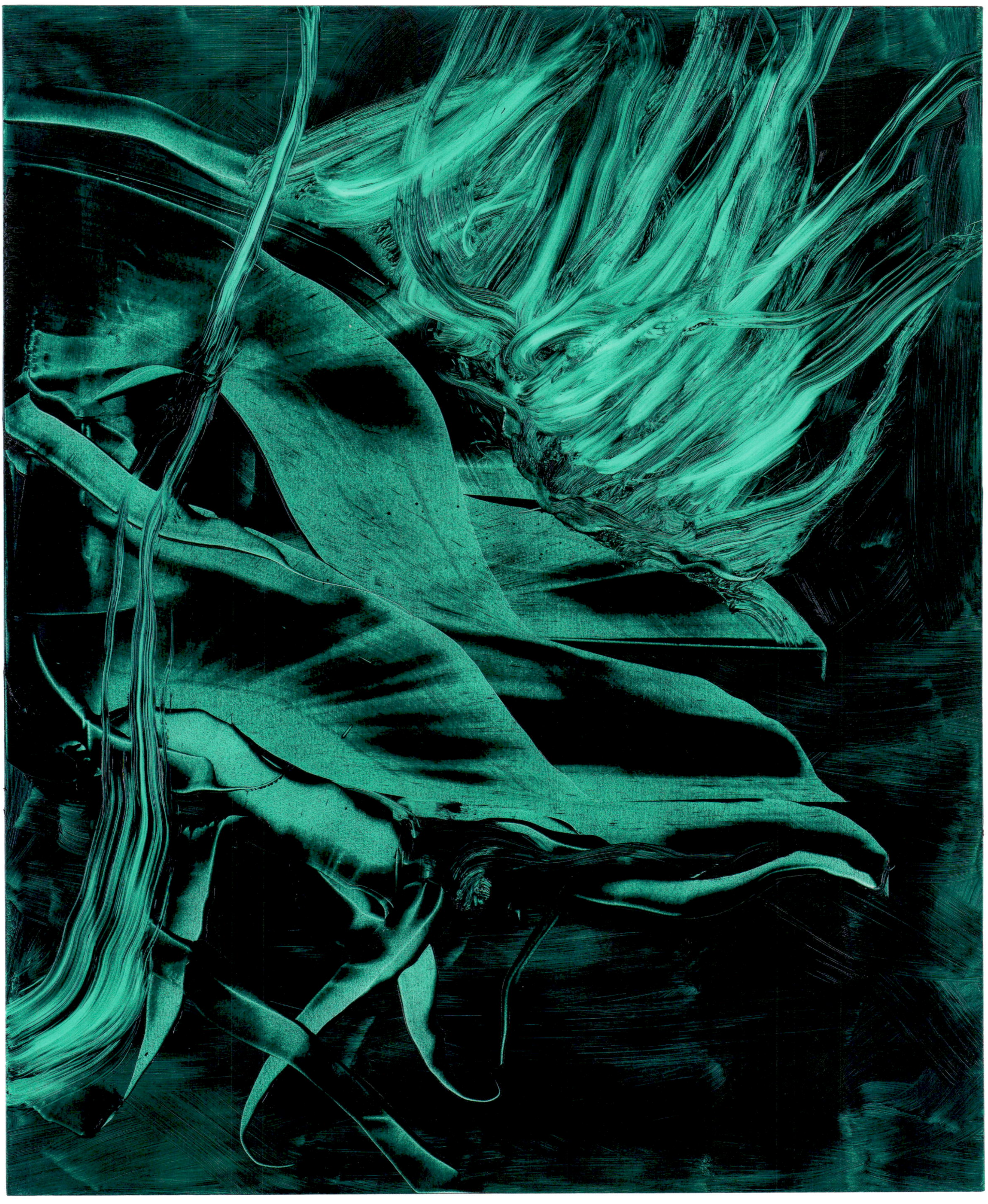

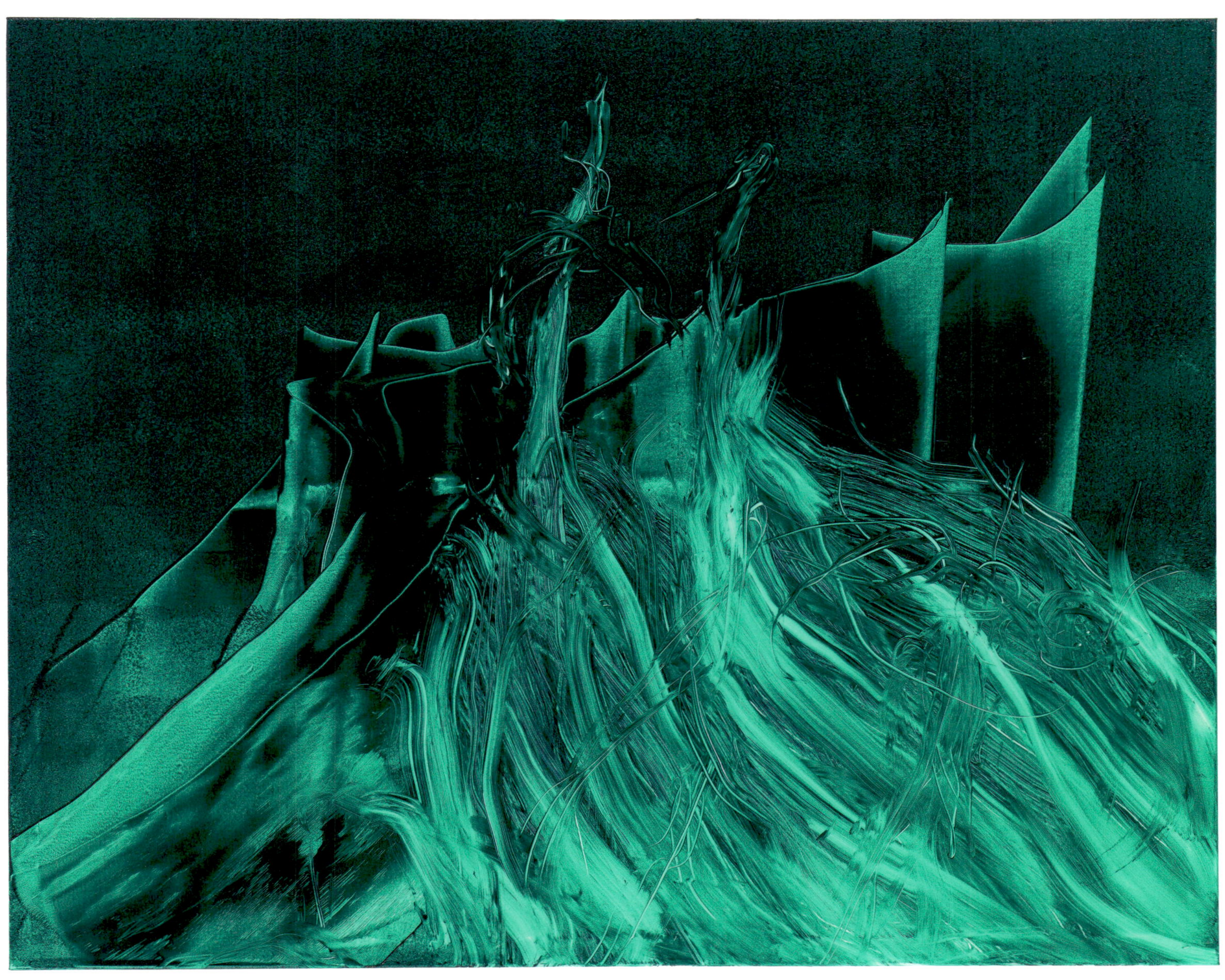

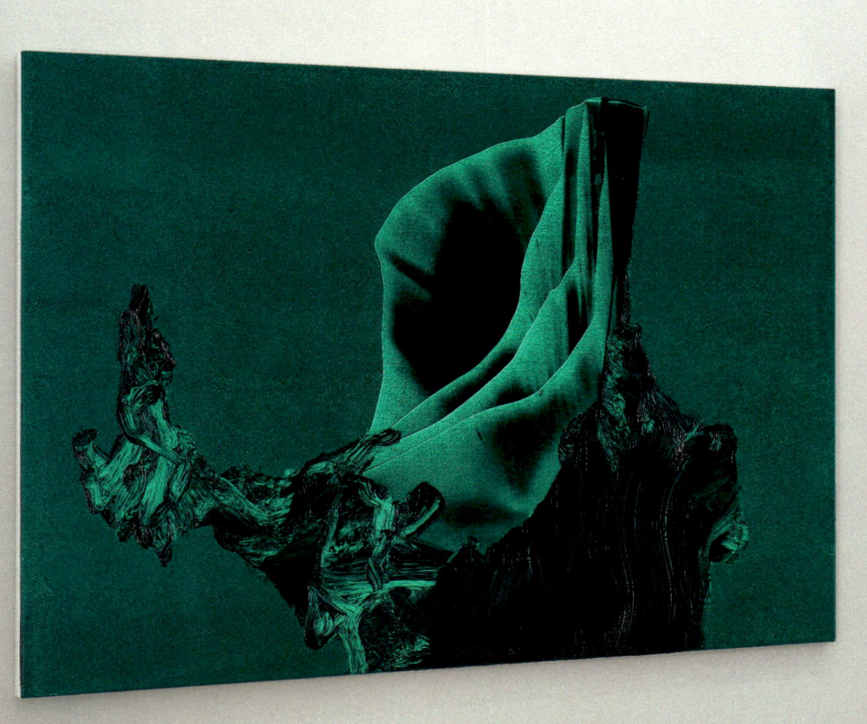

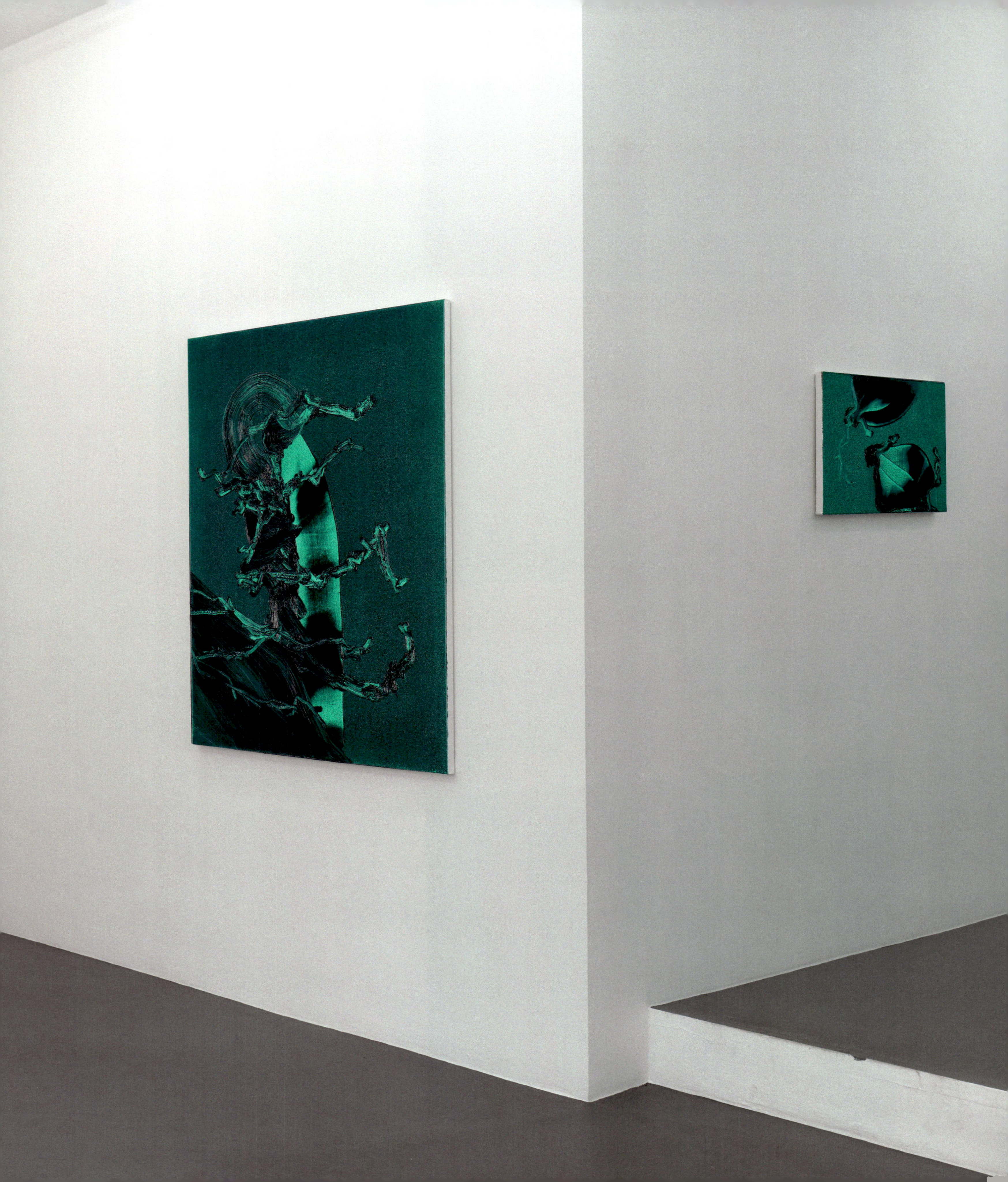

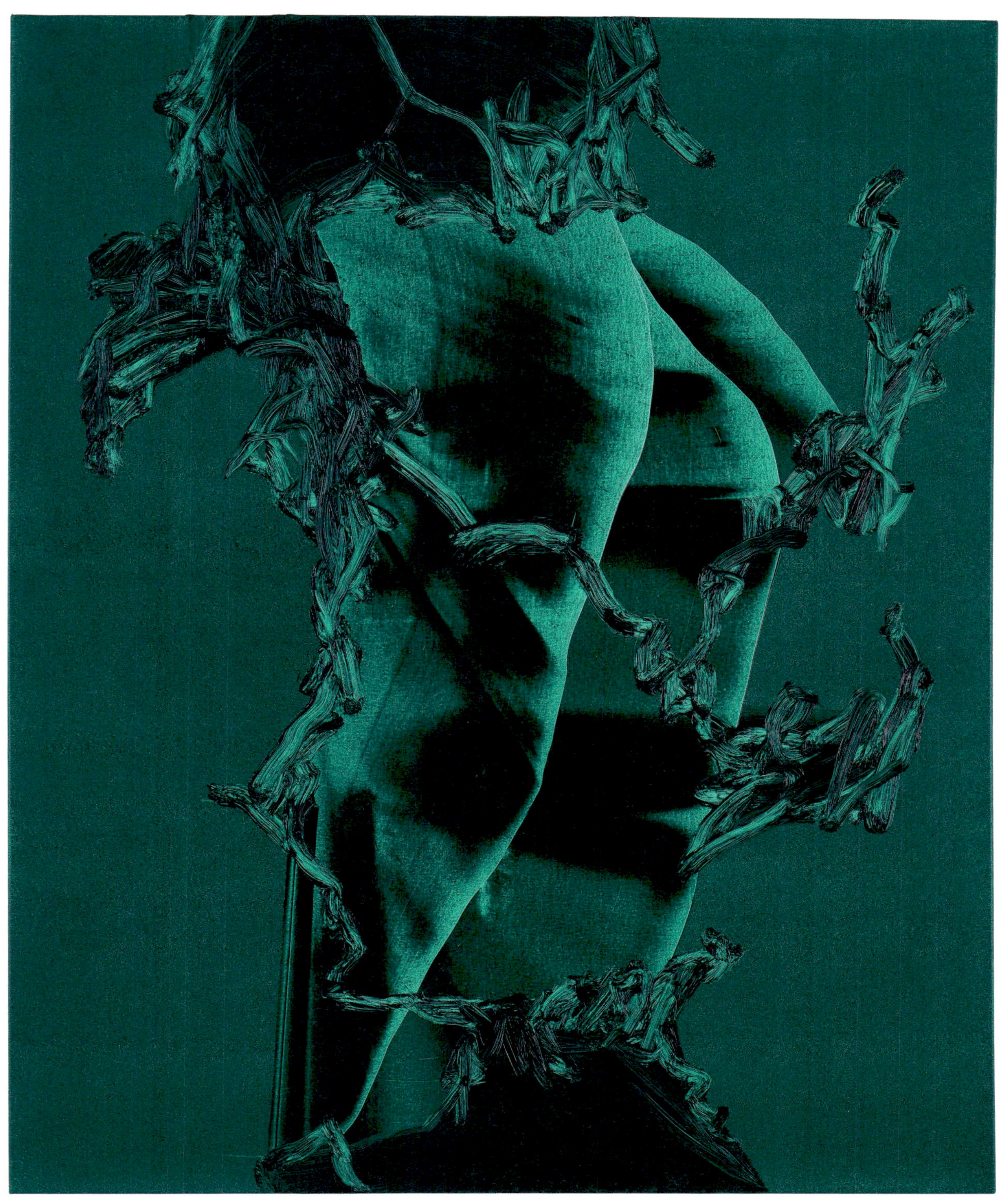

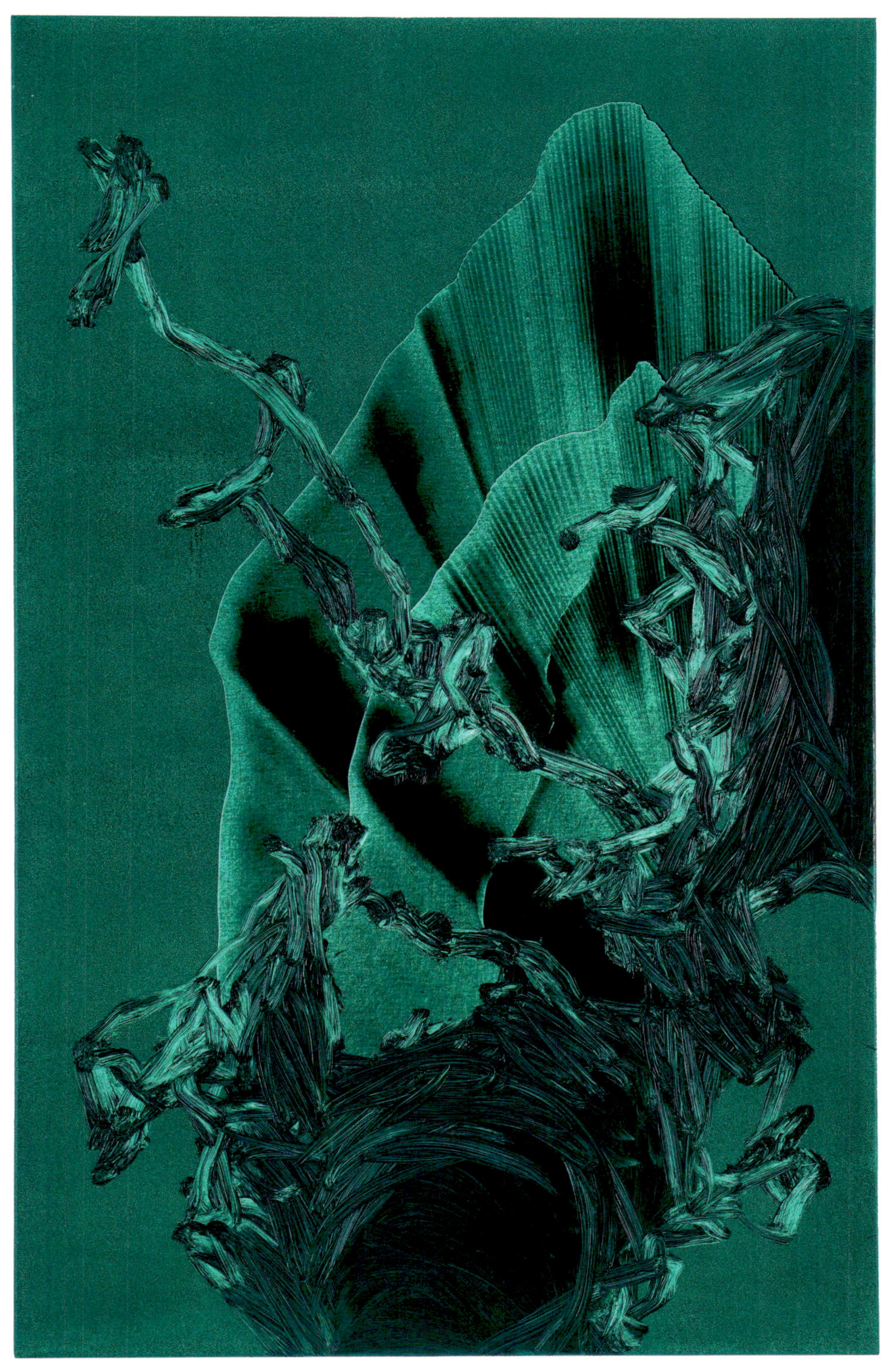

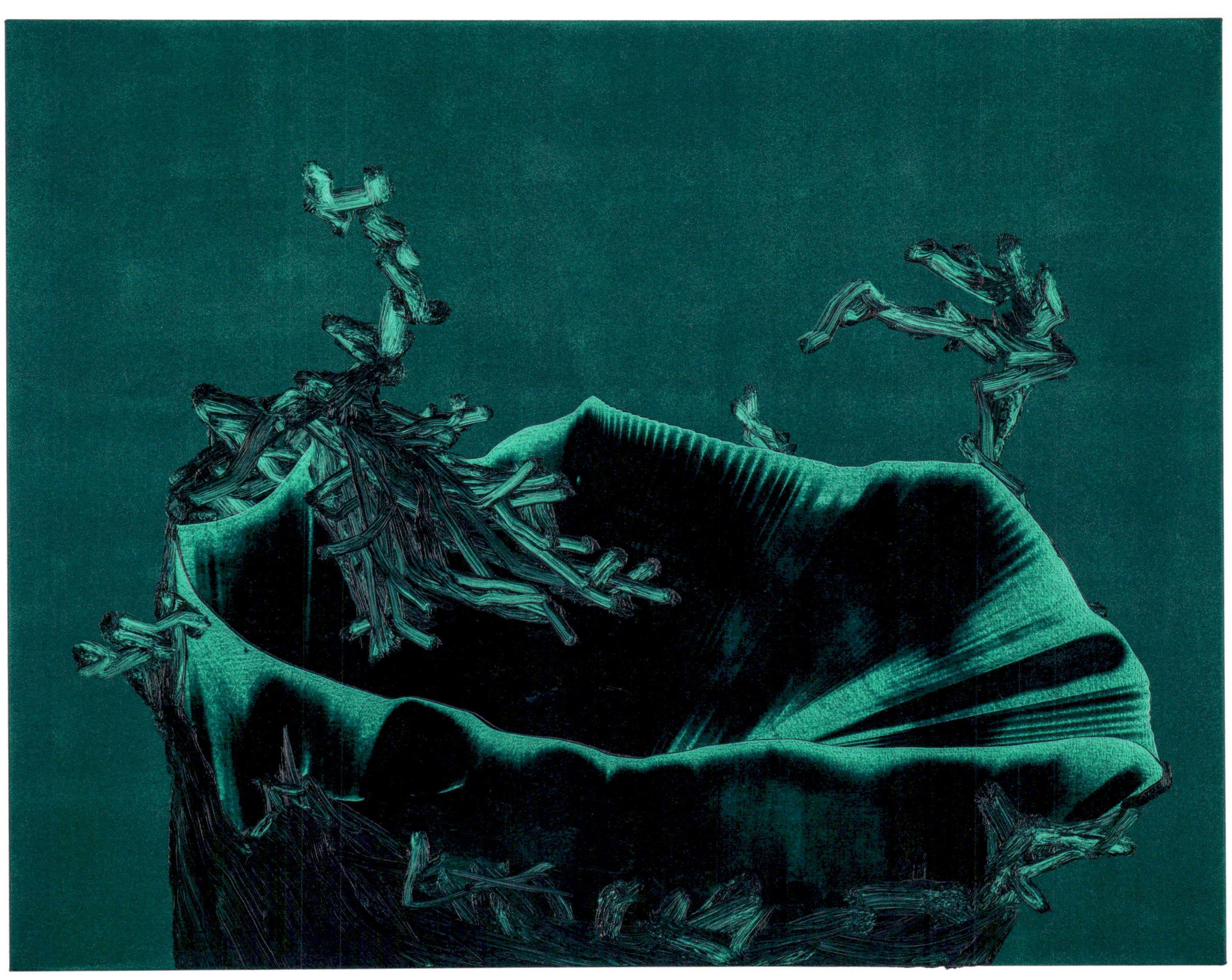

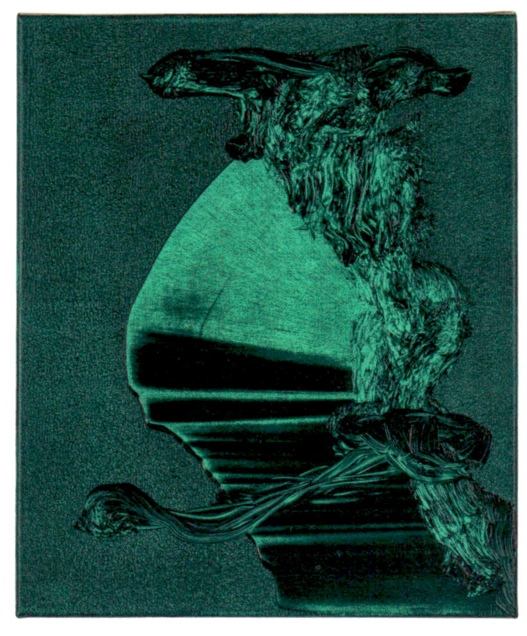

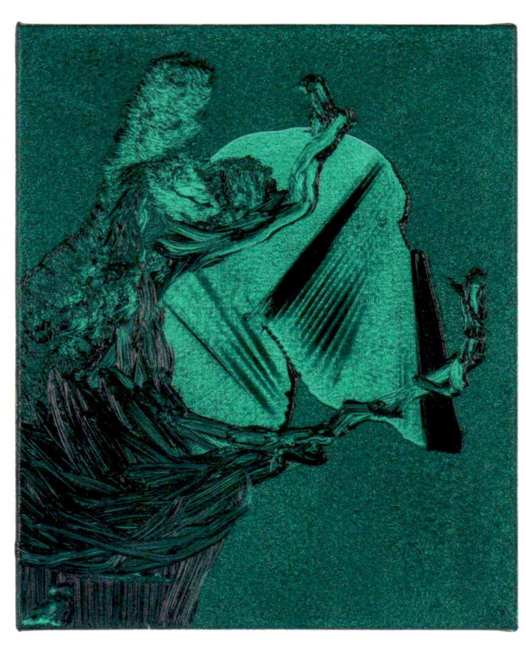

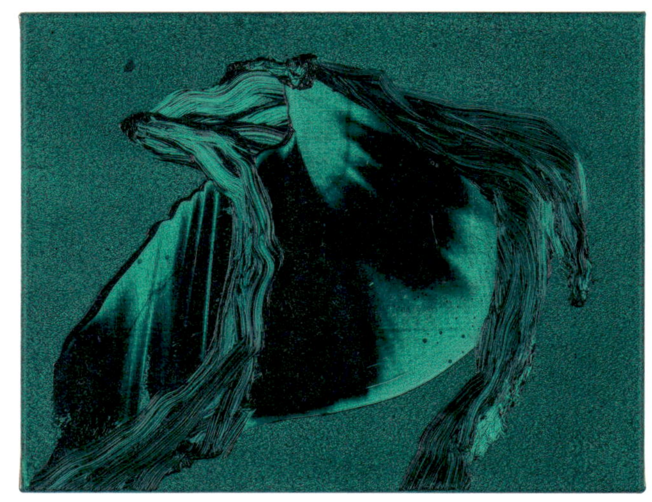

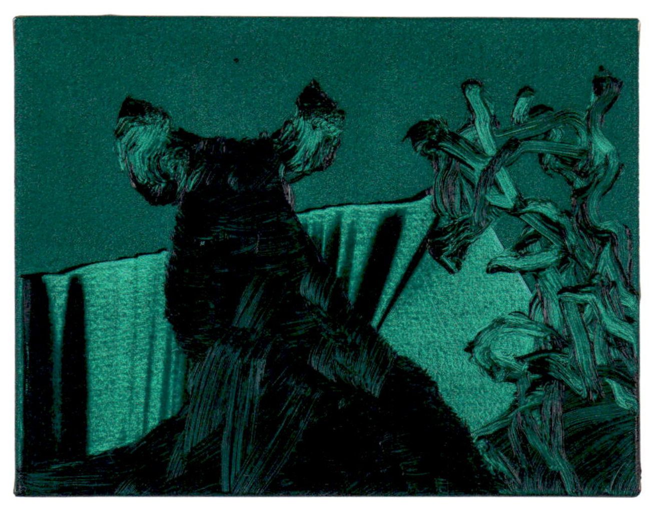

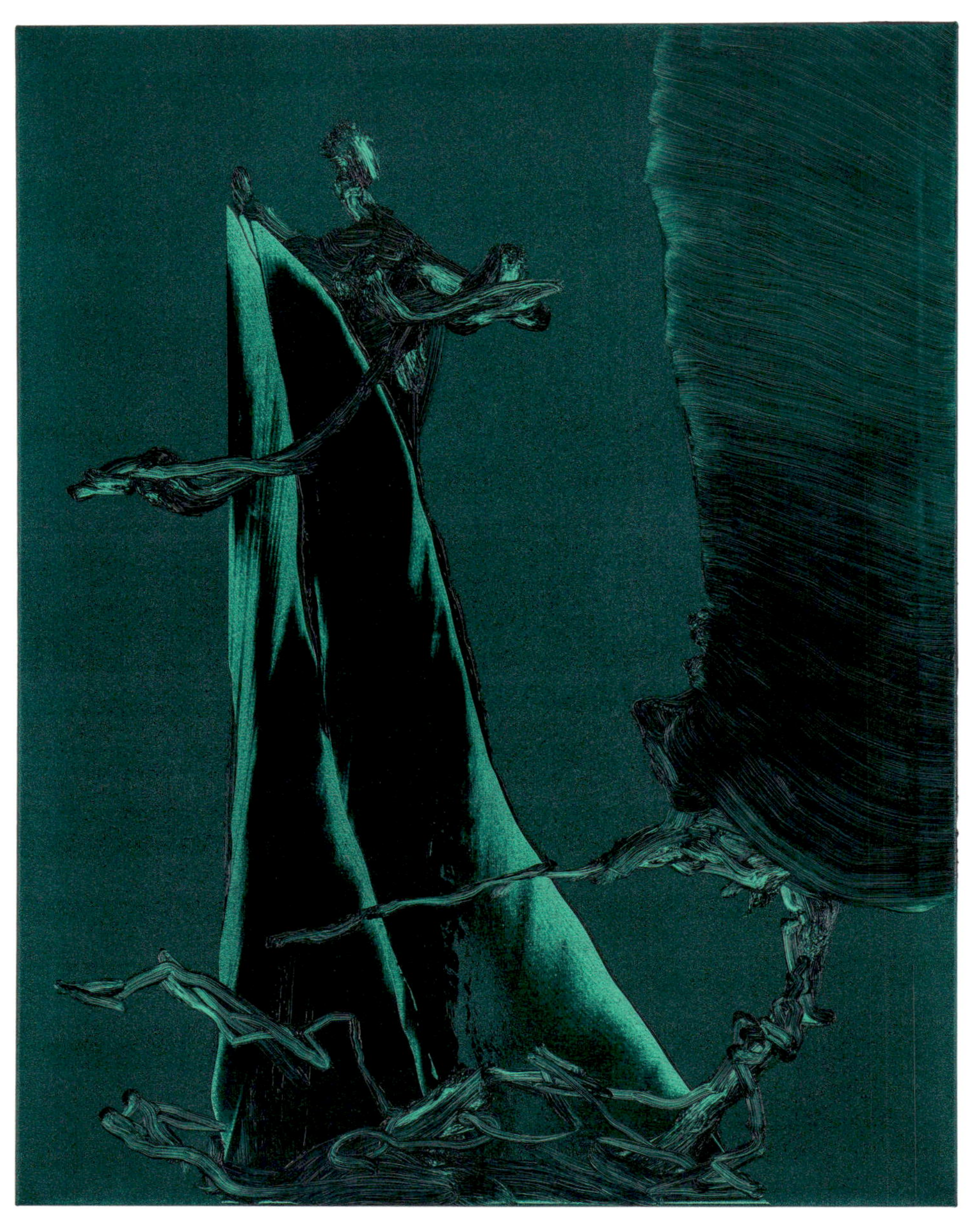

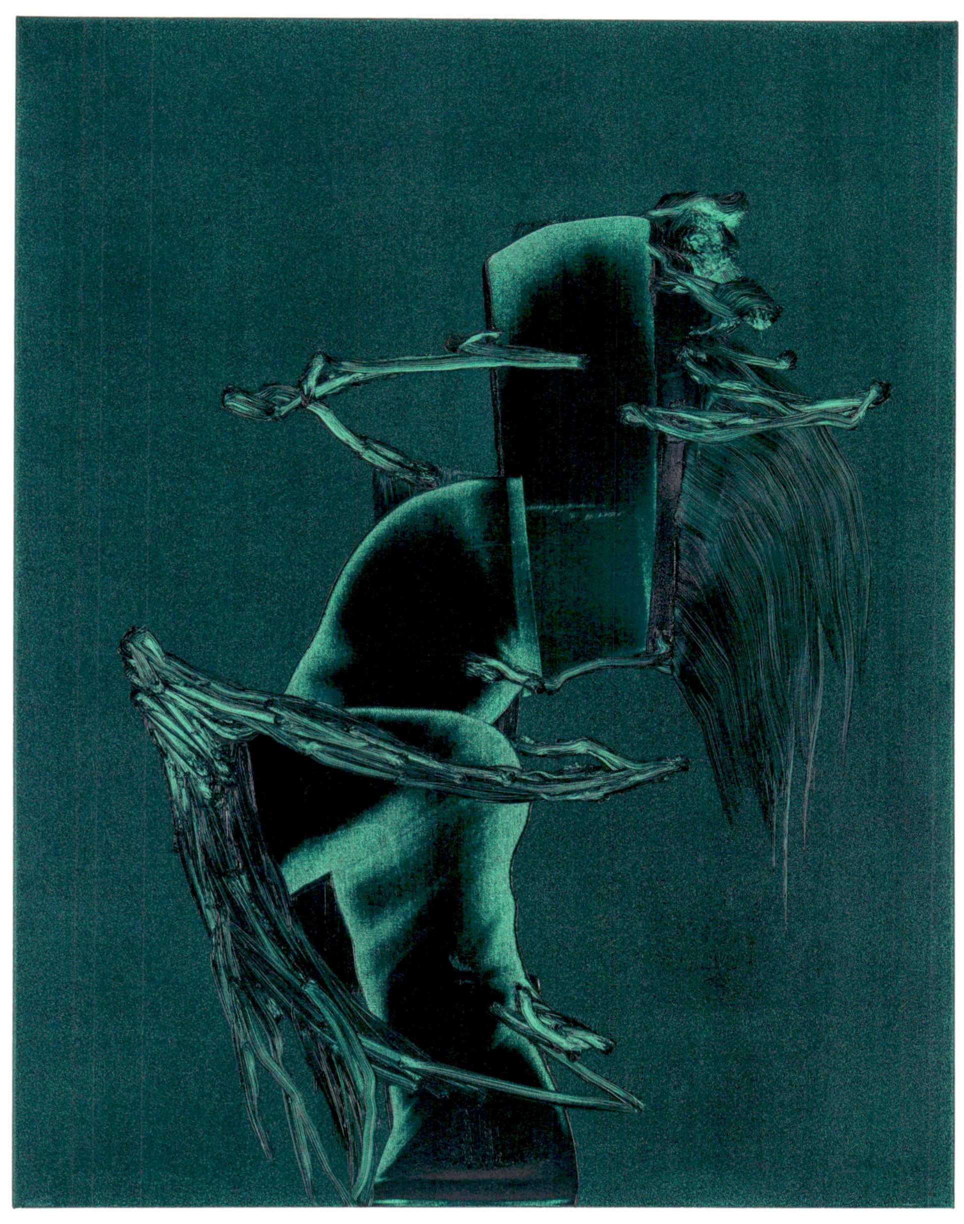

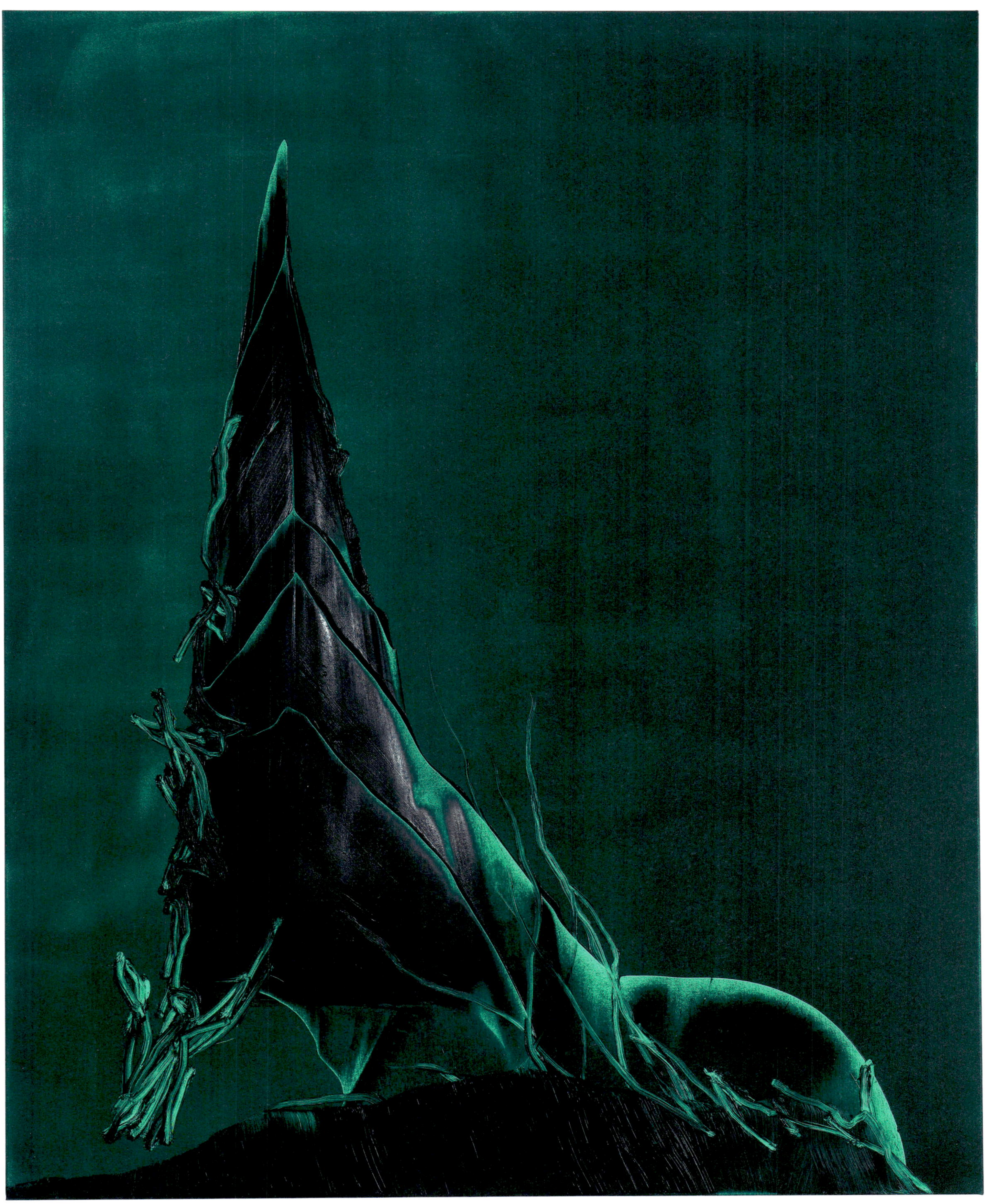

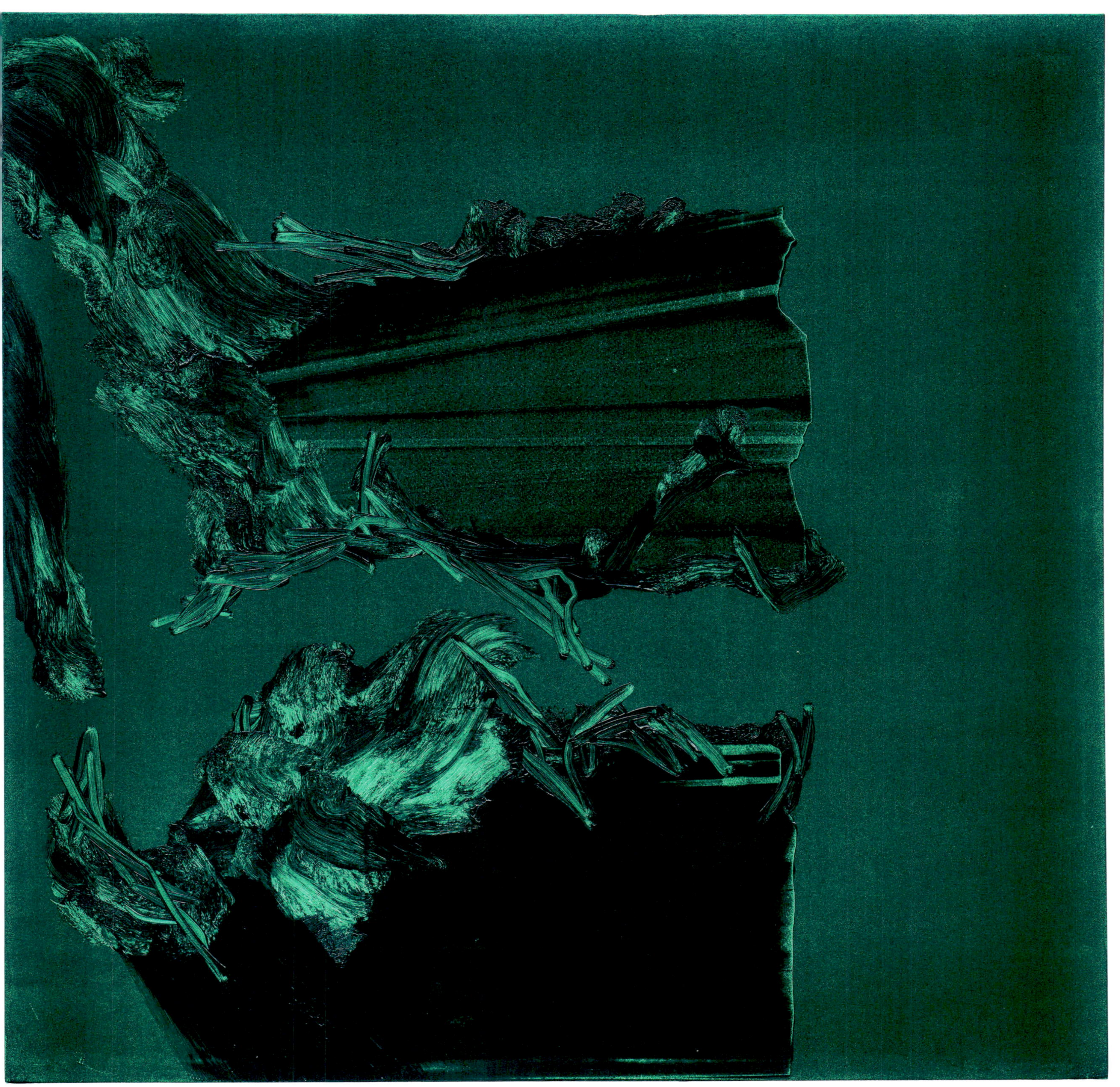

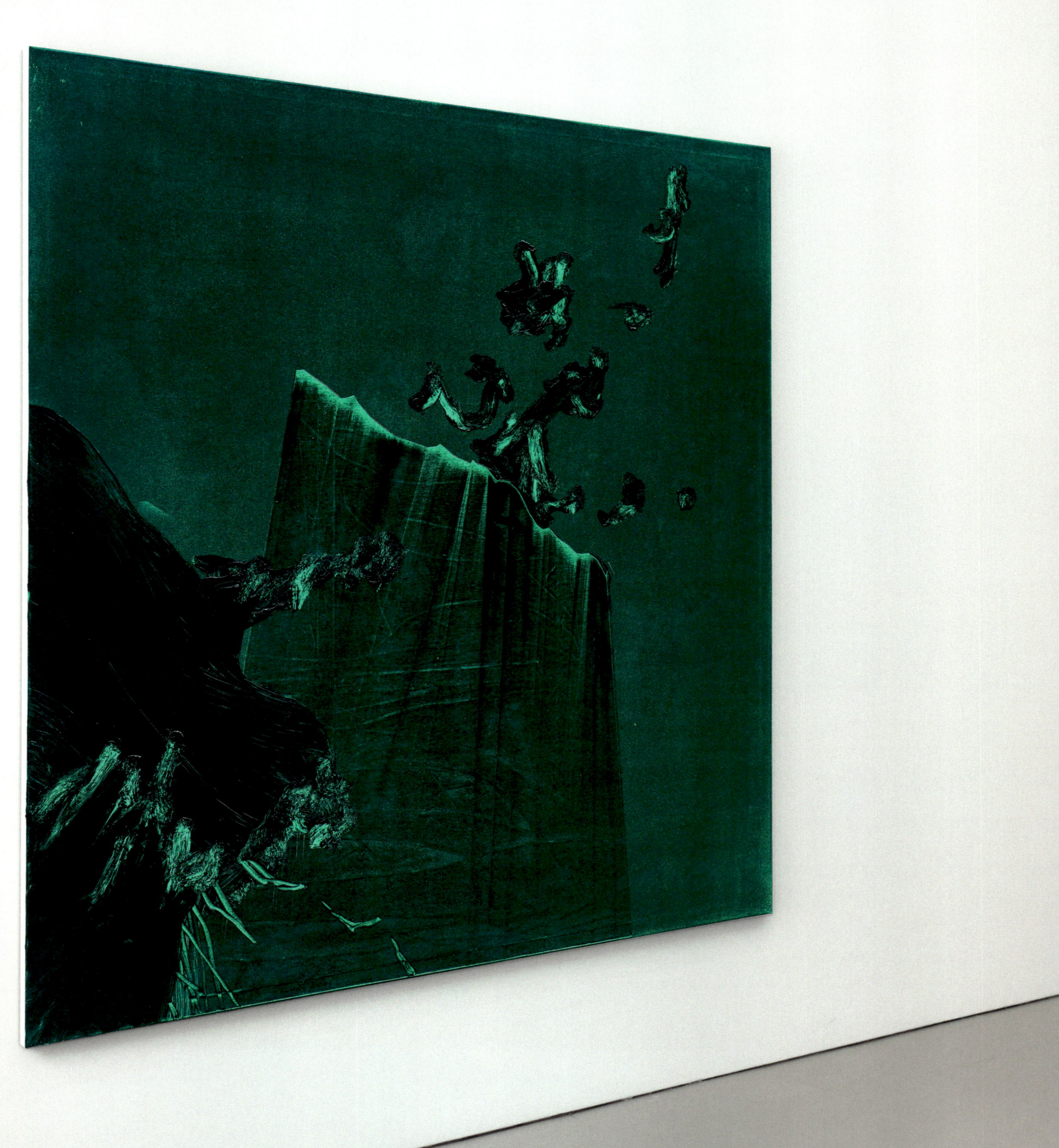

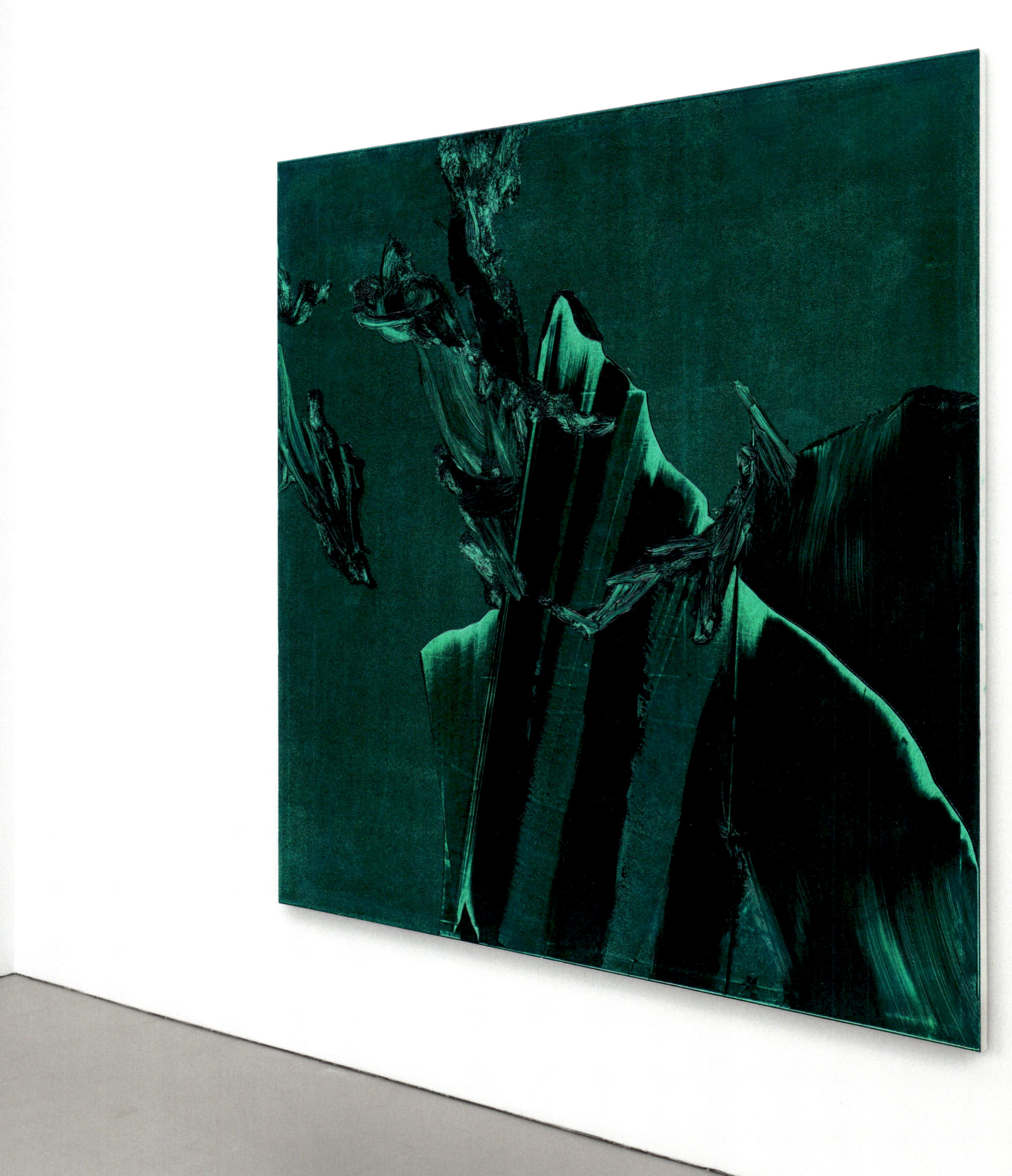

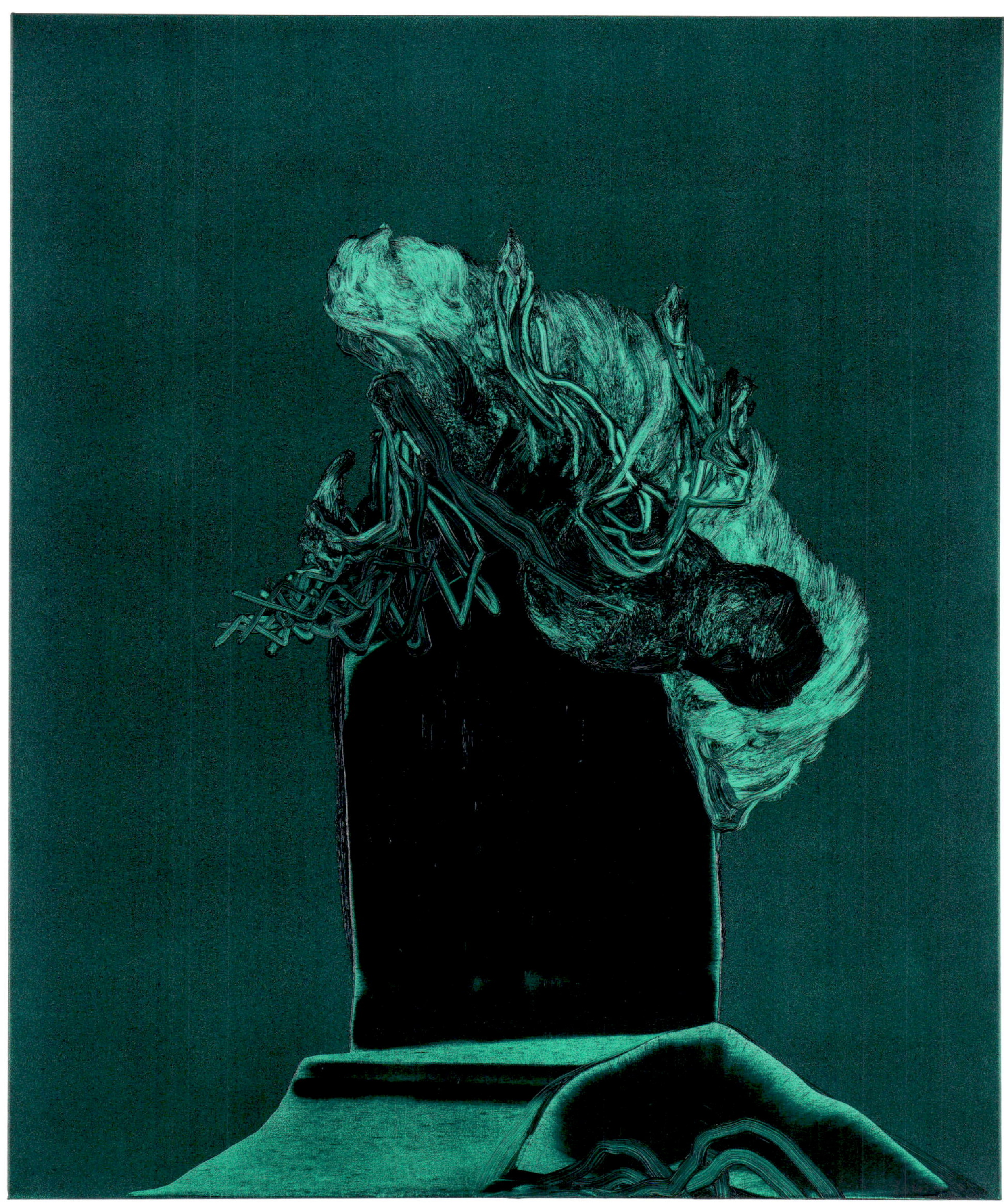

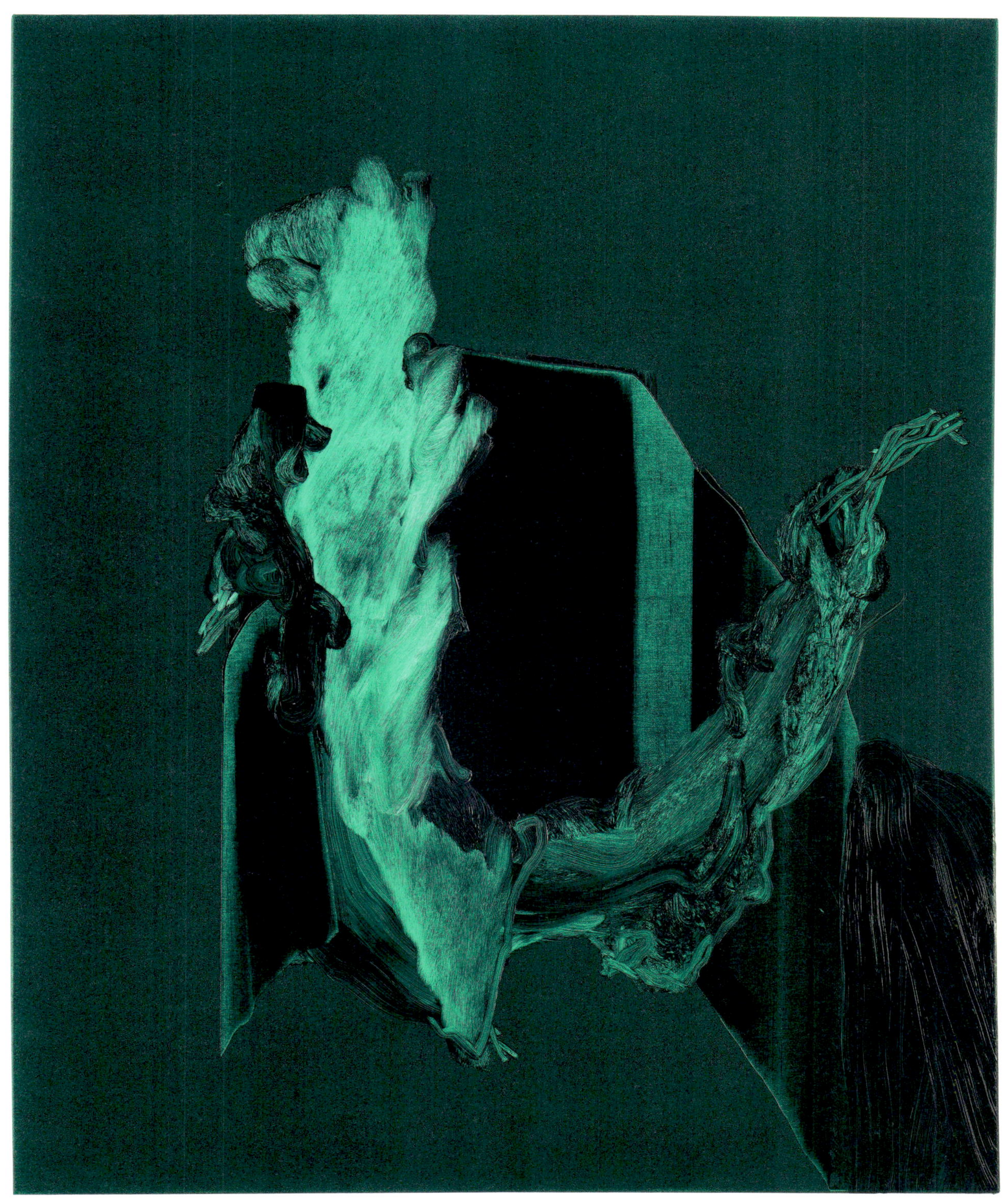

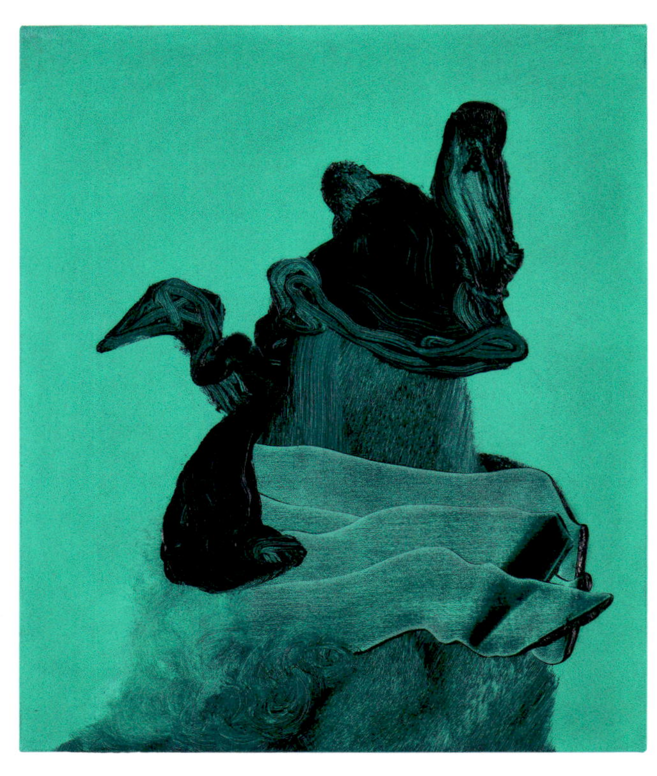

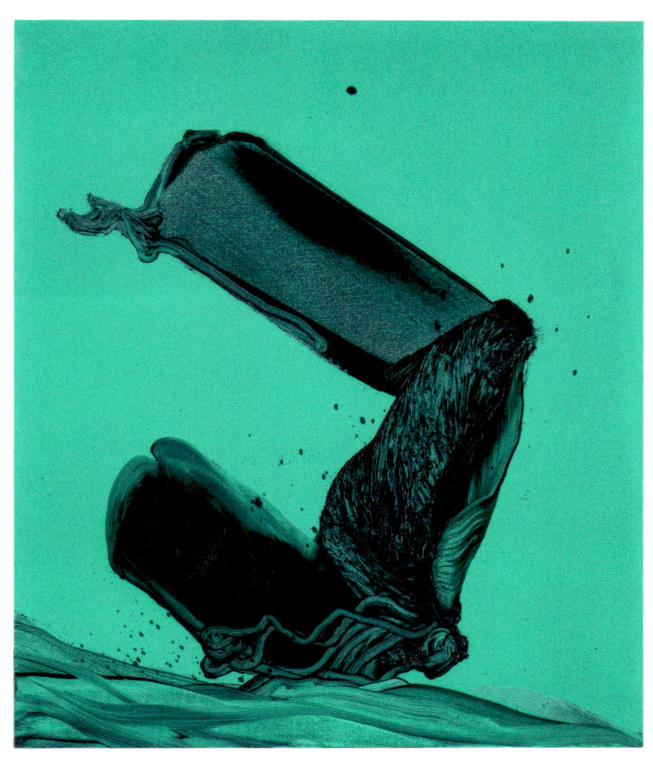

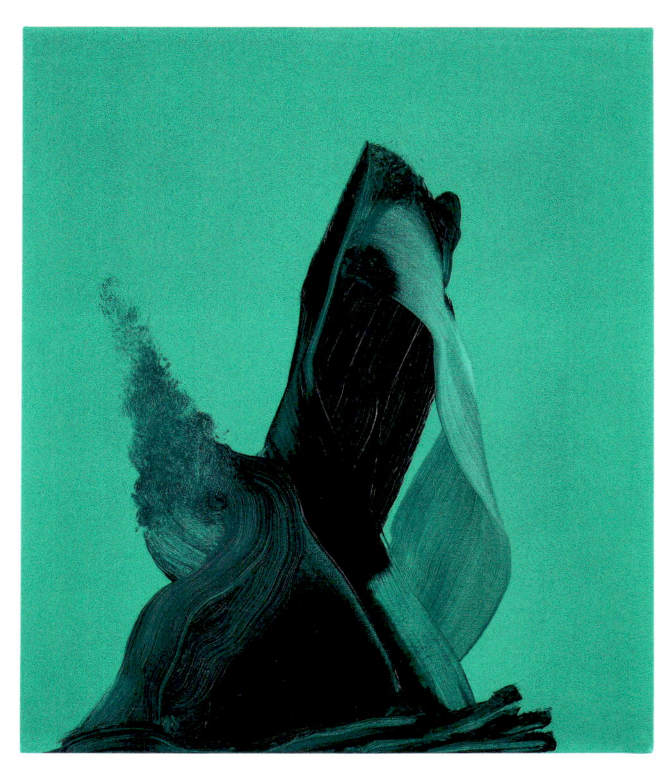

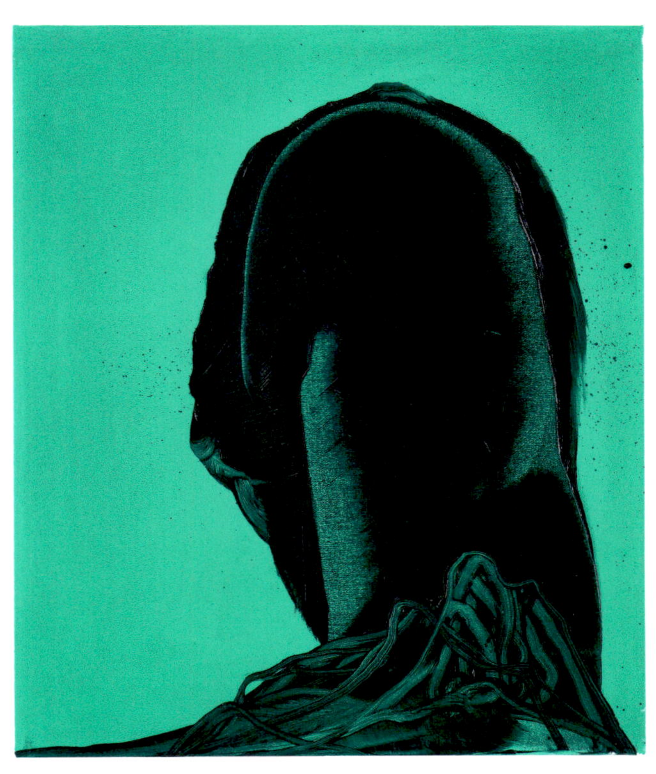

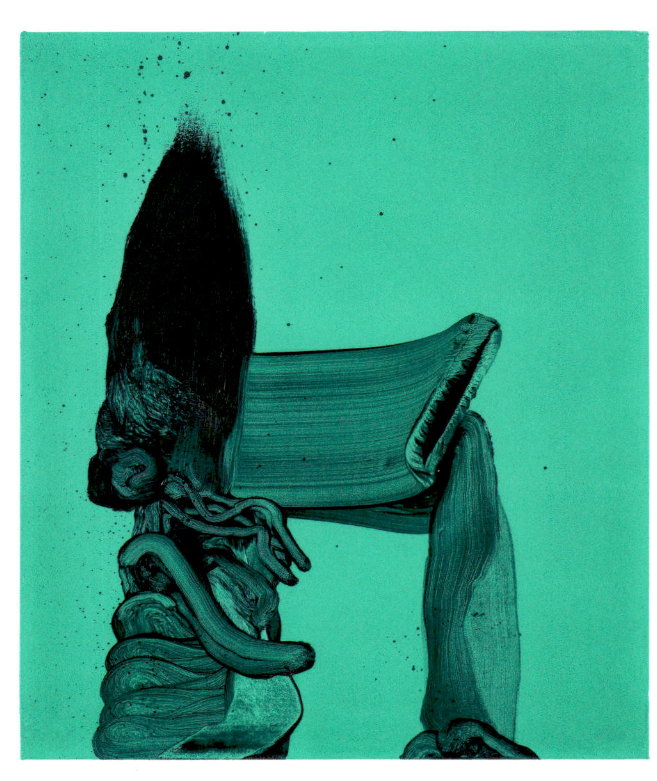

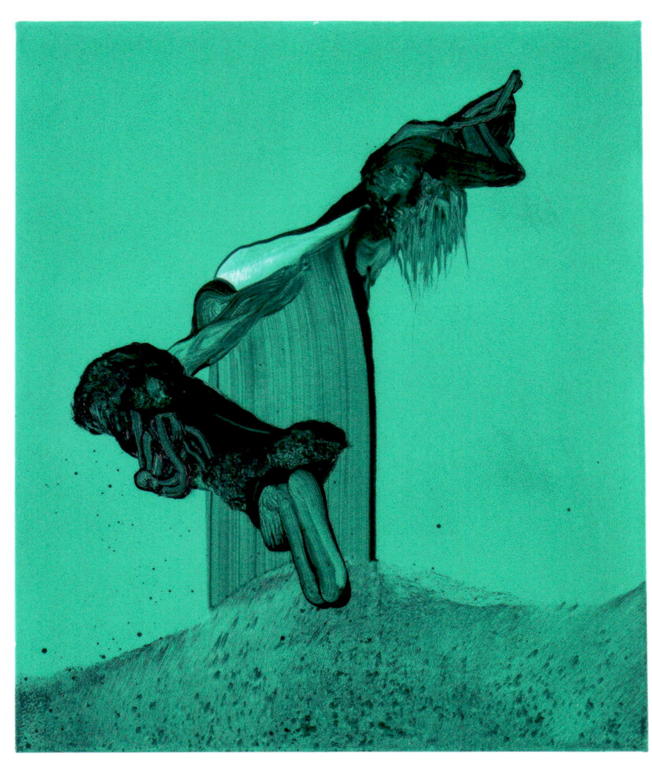

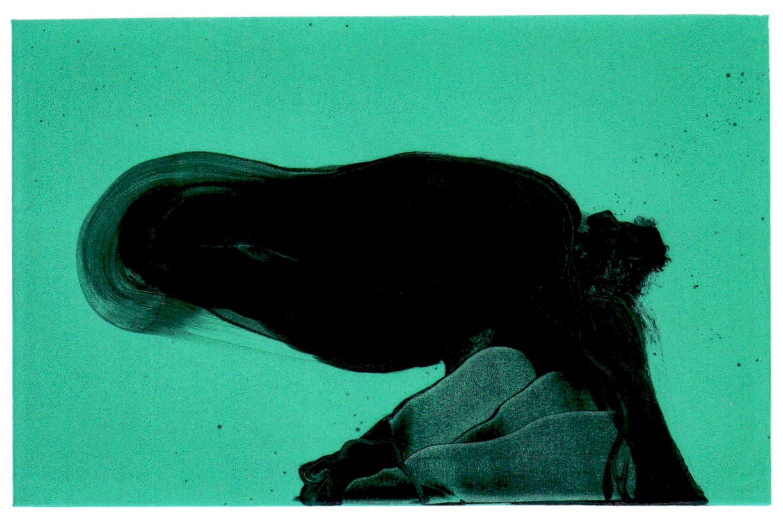

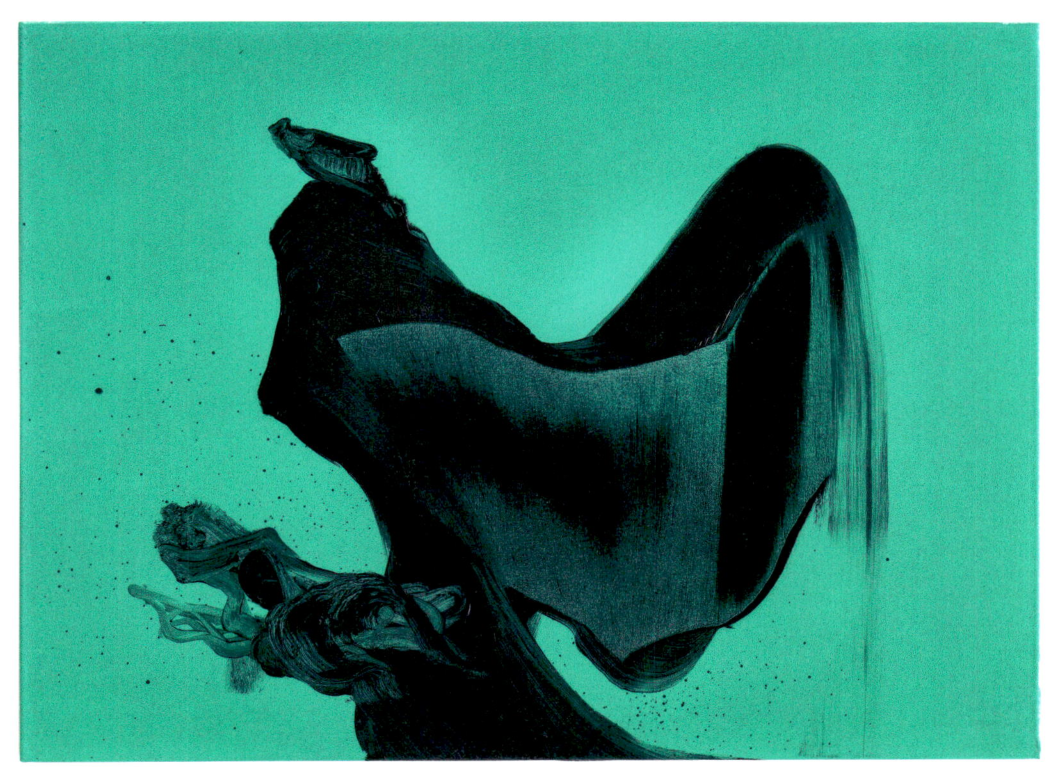

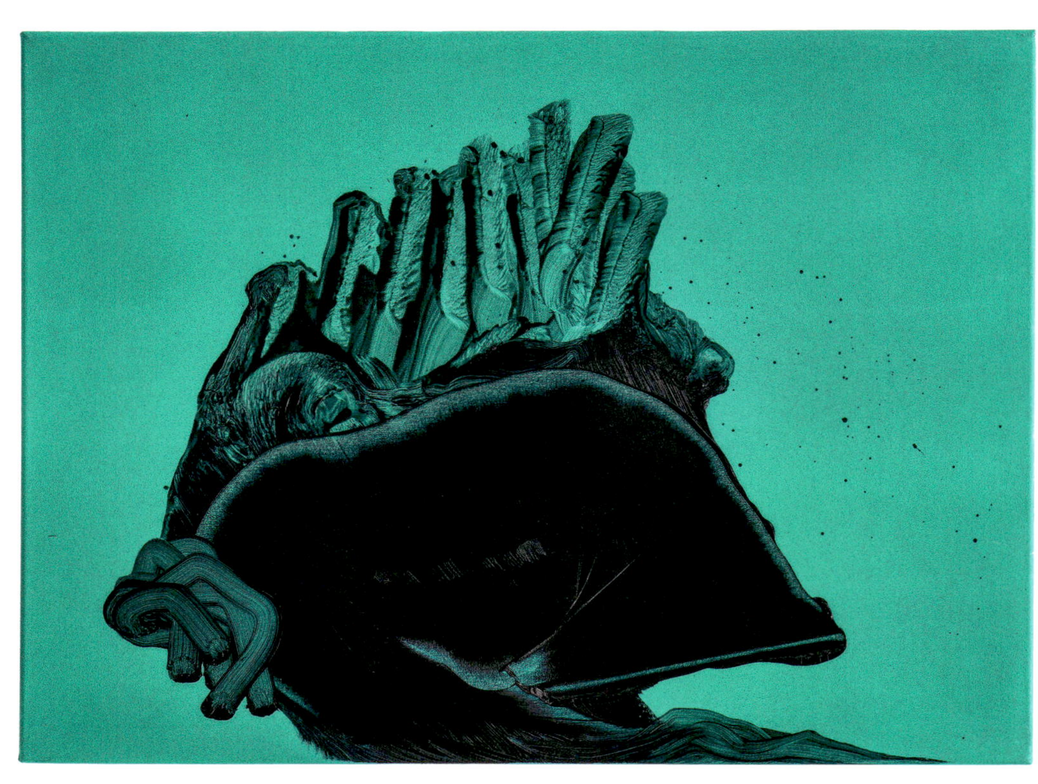

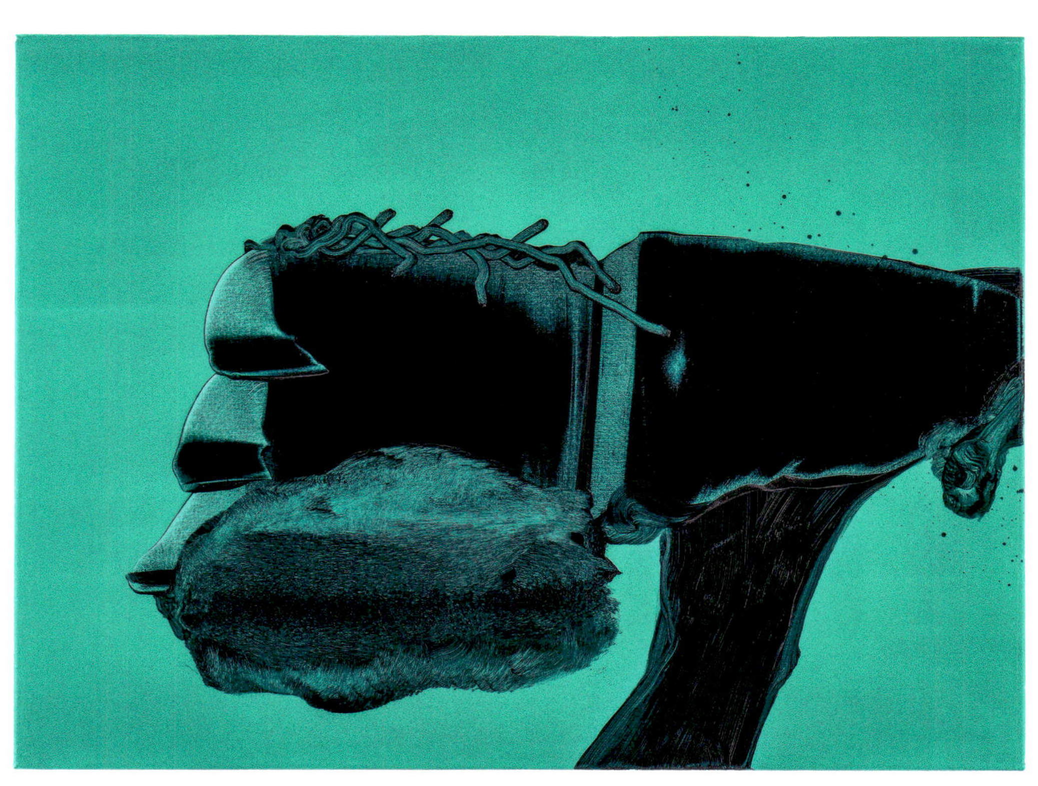

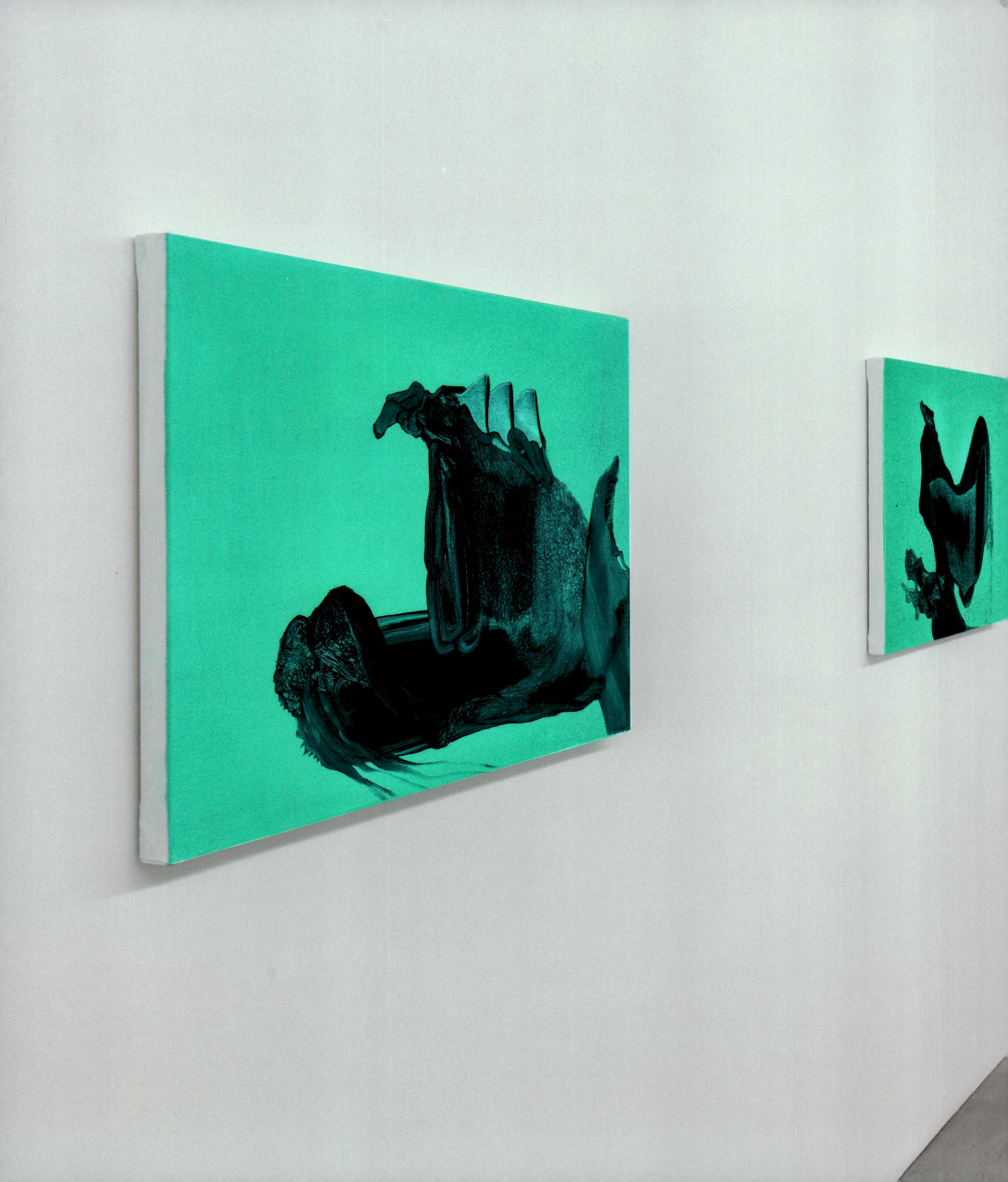

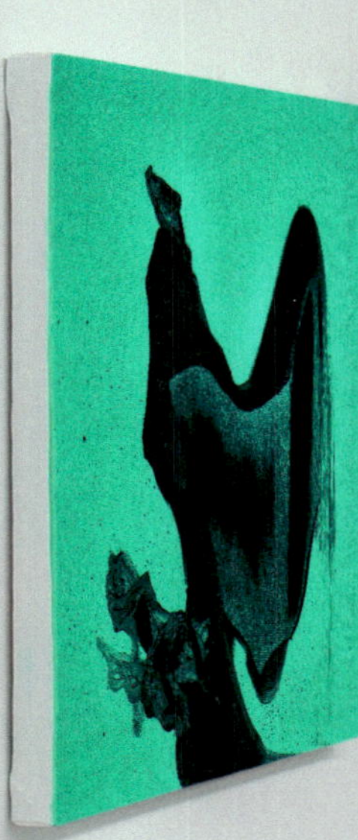

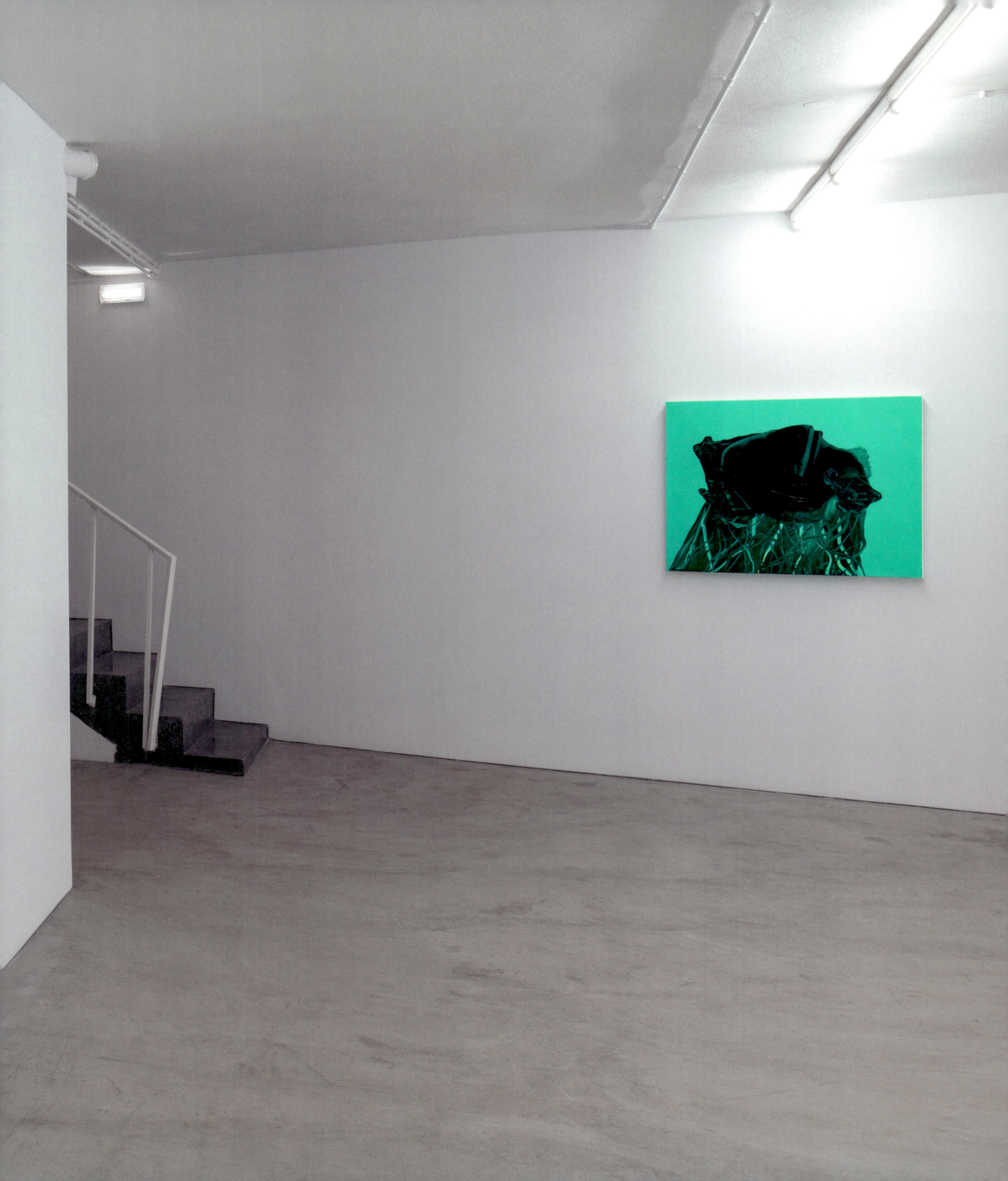

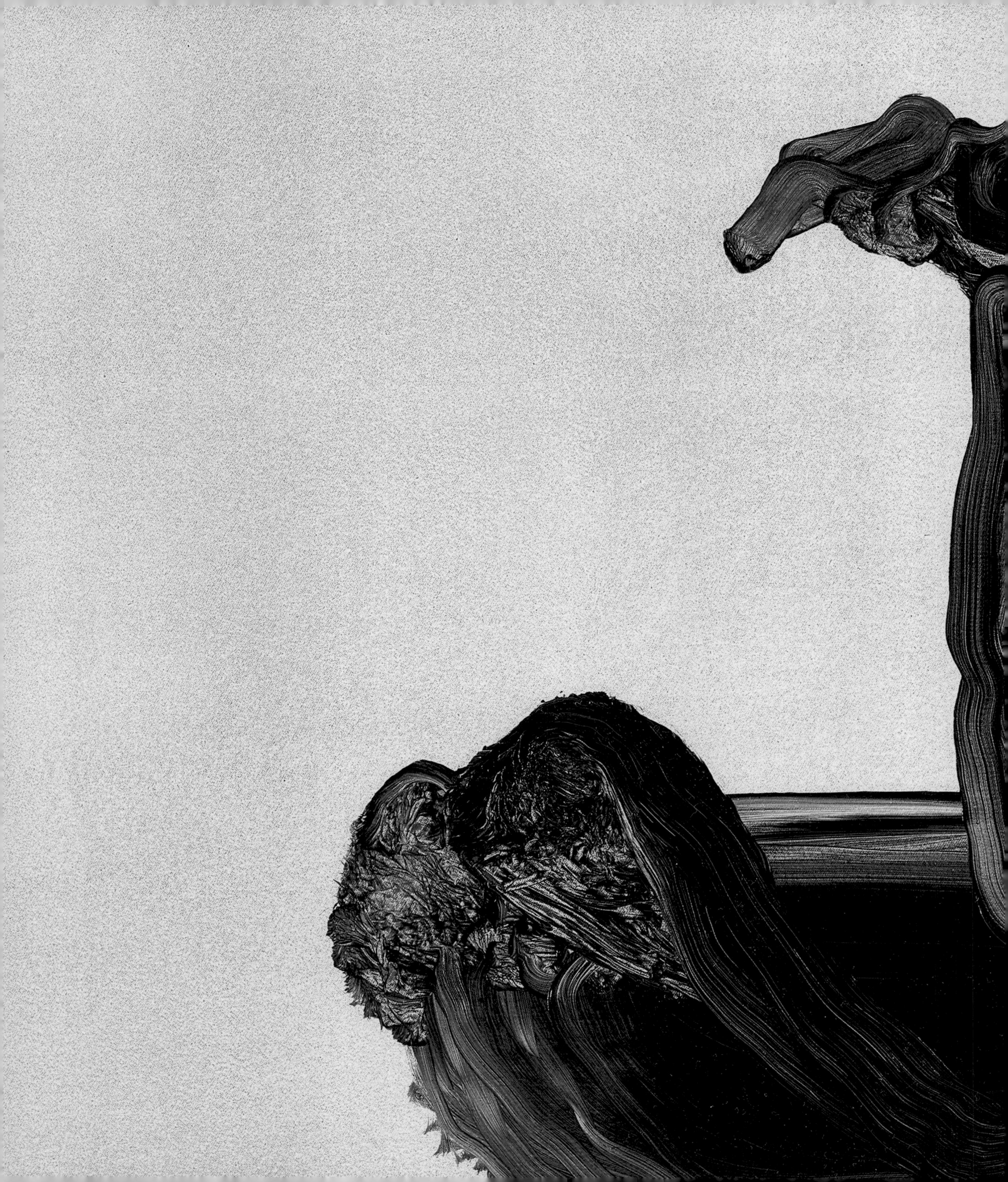

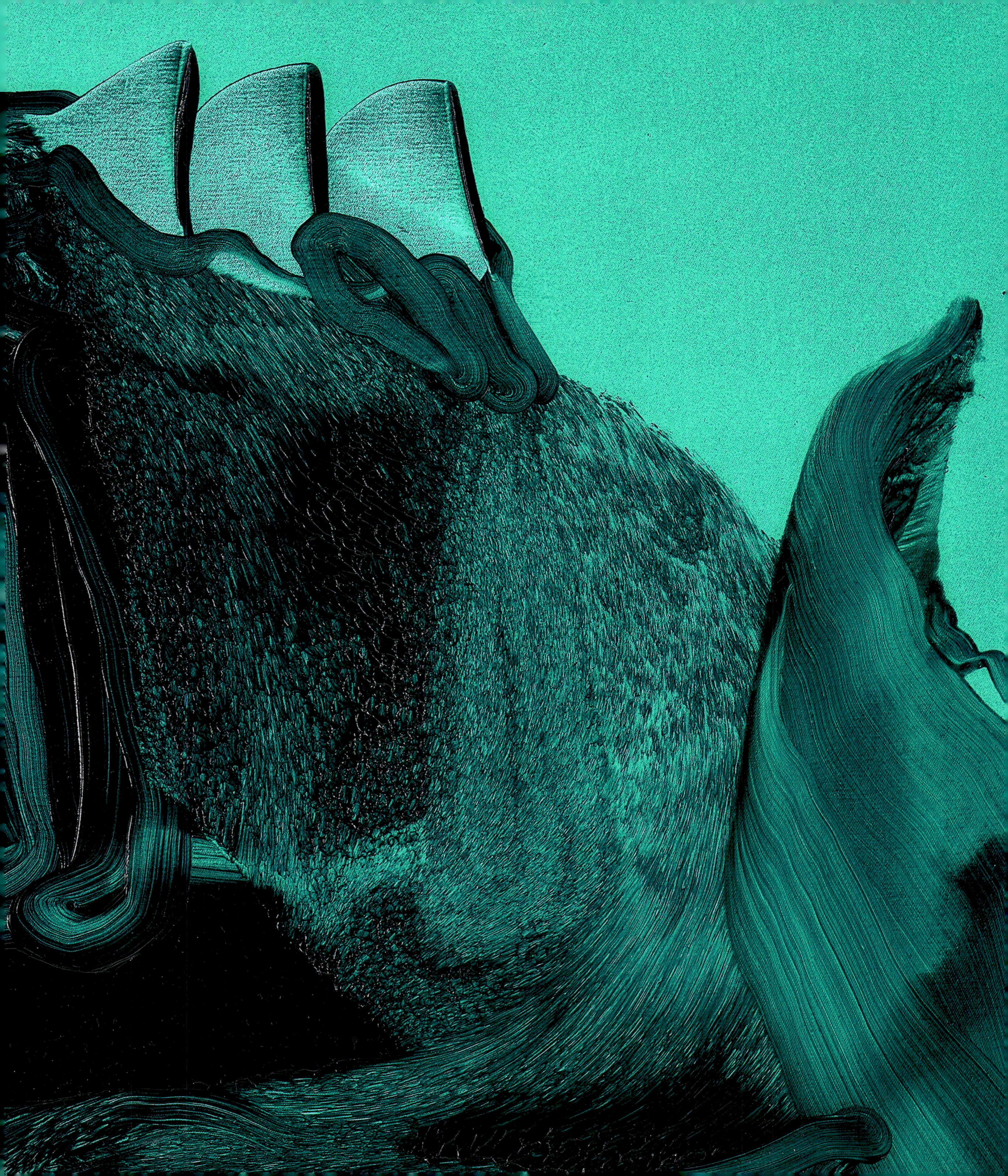

Über Grün

Peter Lodermeyer

»Grün« – das wäre wohl, ganz kurz und knapp, die Antwort, die man am häufigsten erhielte, wenn man Besucher der jüngsten Ausstellungen von Daniel Lergon danach fragte, wie denn seine neuen Bilder aussähen. Dass sie grün sind, charakterisiert sie in der Tat, entfalten sie doch geradezu ein Übermaß, ja einen Exzess an Grün, insbesondere wenn man eine größere Anzahl dieser Arbeiten in Ausstellungen nebeneinander sieht. Ihr Grünsein verbindet die einzelnen Bilder über Formatunterschiede und Wandabstände hinweg und lässt sie wie Ausschnitte einer ganz eigenen, durchaus fremdartigen Bildwelt erscheinen. Dass Ölfarbe als Material im Zentrum seiner Bilder steht, ist ein überraschend neues Moment in Lergons Werk. Wenn man seine früheren Arbeiten ebenso prägnant mit ein, zwei Worten charakterisieren wollte, würde man bei seinen Gemälden auf retroreflektiven Leinwänden wohl zunächst deren Veränderlichkeit in der Anschauung hervorheben, bei den Wandarbeiten mit Metallpigmenten die stumpfe, trockene Materialität der Farbsubstanzen und bei seiner Malerei mit angesäuertem Wasser auf Metallgrundierung die sich aus den chemischen Prozessen ergebenden Strukturen. Die grünen Bilder haben allerdings sowohl mit den retroreflektiven Gemälden als auch mit denen auf Metallgrundierungen gemeinsam, dass der Malgrund eine herausragende Rolle spielt, wie schon der Titel *Unter Grün* andeutet. In den früheren Bildern bestimmte der Einfluss des Hintergrunds – der retroreflektiven Leinwand beziehungsweise der Metalle – physikalisch oder chemisch hervorgerufene Licht- und Farbeffekte. Bei den grünen Bildern dient der Malgrund als eine Art Reflektor: Er bringt die variierende Dichte des aufgetragenen Malmaterials zur Erscheinung.

Nach seinen Untersuchungen ungewöhnlicher Werkstoffe und Oberflächen steht in Lergons grünen Bildern – sie entstehen seit Ende 2015 – Farbe als Farbe im Mittelpunkt, anschaulich gemacht in einem klassischen malerischen Medium: Öl auf Leinwand. Es scheint, als ob der Künstler die Erfahrungen aus seinen jahrelangen Experimenten mit neuen Malmitteln und Bildträgern auf eine traditionelle Malweise anwenden und dabei austesten wolle. Tatsächlich erforscht er in seinen grünen Bildern die Ölfarbe eben auch als Material und keineswegs nur als Kolorit; die Farbe Grün ist bei ihm sowohl »colour« als auch »paint«. Die koloristischen Abstufungen und Helligkeitsnuancen, die in diesen Bildern verblüffende Wirkungen zeigen, ergeben sich nämlich – das bemerkt man erst auf den zweiten, genaueren Blick – unmittelbar aus den Materialeigenschaften der einzigen verwendeten Ölfarbe: Phthalogrün. Dieses spezifische Grün wird durch die unterschiedliche Dichte des Auftrags hervorgehoben, wobei seine Wirkungsweise erheblich davon abhängt, ob es auf weißem oder neongelbem Untergrund appliziert wird.

Man mag als Betrachter zunächst kaum glauben, dass es wirklich nur eine einzige Farbe ist, die in diesen Bildern zum Einsatz kommt. Ihre dunkelsten Partien sind keineswegs schwarz, wie es zunächst den Anschein hat, sondern ein tiefes, samtiges Dunkelgrün. Es gehört zu den Materialeigenschaften des

Phthalogrün, dass es eine ungewöhnlich breite Skala an Helligkeitsabstufungen zwischen jenem Beinaheschwarz bei pastosem und einem giftig leuchtenden, blaustichigen Grünton bei stark verdünntem Farbauftrag hervorbringt. Lergon arbeitet die Möglichkeiten und unterschiedlichen Farbabstufungen des Malmaterials heraus und öffnet gewissermaßen die Farbe, indem er ihren Nuancenreichtum ausbreitet. Da er die Bandbreite an Helligkeitswerten mithilfe einer reichen Binnendifferenzierung seiner Motive ausschöpft, kommt man kaum auf den Gedanken, diese Bilder unter der Rubrik »monochrome Malerei« abzuhandeln. Sie erscheinen aufgrund dieses Nuancenreichtums »multimonochrom«, wie man in Anlehnung an den Ausstellungstitel *Multimono* (Galerie Christian Lethert, Köln, 2016) sagen möchte. Zudem arbeiten sie mit dem elementaren Prinzip der Gestaltpsychologie, das in der monochromen Malerei üblicherweise sorgsam vermieden wird: dem Gegensatz von Figur und Grund. Die Vielfalt der Helligkeitswerte in Lergons Bildern und die sich aus ihnen ergebenden illusionistischen Effekte rufen eher den traditionellen Begriff des Chiaroscuro in Erinnerung als den modernen der Monochromie. Es ist ein überaus reizvoller Gedanke, Lergons grüne Bilder als eine Neuinterpretation der Helldunkelmalerei zu sehen, wie sie die Kunst des Barock – man denke etwa an Caravaggio oder Rembrandt – weithin prägte. Das Herausmodellieren der Motive mit Licht und Schatten ist hier ganz auf die unterschiedlichen Grünwerte verlagert und noch enorm gesteigert, wo Lergon statt einer weißen eine neongelbe Grundierung verwendet. Dadurch wird die Licht- und Tiefenwirkung der Bilder erheblich verstärkt. Das Gelb kommt nicht als zweite Farbe zum Einsatz, sondern als lichthaltiger Fond, der die grüne Farbe durchdringt, weiter ins Gelbspektrum treibt und dabei ihre Strahlkraft verstärkt. Nur an den schmalen Bildseiten kann sich das Gelb als solches entfalten und aufgrund der Reflexion des Umgebungslichts eine leuchtende Aura rund um die Bilder an die Wände zaubern.

Das Herausmodellieren der Bildmotive – falls man überhaupt von »Motiven« sprechen kann – geschieht durch den Einsatz verschiedener Instrumente beim Auftragen und Verteilen der Farbe. Je nachdem, ob und wie Lergon die Farbe mit schmalem Pinsel appliziert, mit Schwämmen aufträgt oder mit Rakeln und Spachteln verwischt beziehungsweise wieder von der Fläche schabt, ergeben sich deutliche Unterschiede in Helligkeit und Textur, sodass sich eine verwirrende Wirkung von Tiefenillusion und Räumlichkeit einstellt – eine Räumlichkeit, die gleichwohl nicht homogen, sondern inkonsistent ausfällt und das Auge mit der Gestaltbildung, das heißt mit dem Versuch, das Gesehene in eine stimmige räumliche Ordnung zu bringen, beschäftigt (und zugleich überfordert). Da Lergon diesen »Motiven« immer ausreichend unstrukturierte, homogen mit der Rolle aufgetragene Flächen zur Seite gibt, erscheinen sie stets als »Figuren« vor dem jeweiligen Hintergrund. Man kann dabei insgesamt vier verschiedene Bildtypen unterscheiden, je nachdem, ob die Grundierung in Weiß oder Neongelb gehalten und ob der Bildhintergrund hell oder dunkel ausgeführt, das heißt: mit sehr dünn oder sehr dick aufgetragenem Phthalogrün-Pigment gemalt ist. Vor dunklen Hintergründen heben sich die »Figuren« hell, geradezu lichtdurchtränkt ab. Ist das Hintergrundgrün nur dünn auf weißer Grundierung aufgetragen, erscheint die Hintergrundfläche türkisgrün, auf leuchtend gelber Grundierung eher grasgrün, und die dunkleren Motive davor heben sich umso plastischer ab. In diesen Fällen wird unmittelbar deutlich, wie sehr ihr Erscheinungsbild von der Grundierung und der Helligkeit des Hintergrunds abhängt.

Grün ist eine Farbe, die man fast unvermeidlich mit Pflanzen, Natur und Landschaft in Verbindung bringt. Doch das Phthalogrün, das Lergon verwendet, wirkt eigentümlich kühl und bringt in die Naturvorstellung eine gewisse begrifflich schwer zu fassende Fremdheit ein, eine emotionale

Dissonanz. Grund dafür ist sicherlich die Tatsache, dass das Pigment, nämlich Phthalocyaningrün, künstlich erzeugt ist. Es ist ein Produkt der chemischen Industrie und wird erst seit 1938 hergestellt. Schaut man sich die komplexe chemische Strukturformel an, so sieht man, dass im Mittelpunkt der Moleküle jeweils ein Kupferatom sitzt, das von Natrium- und Chlorringen umgeben ist. So steht das Farbmaterial mit seinem Kupferanteil also auch chemisch in der Nähe von Lergons früheren Arbeiten mit Kupfergrundierung.

Die schiere Präsenz der eigentümlichen Farbigkeit des Phthalogrün löst beim Betrachten unweigerlich inhaltliche Vorstellungen aus. So kann man die Arbeiten auf weißer Grundierung zum Beispiel mit Unterwasserwelten assoziieren, jene auf neongelbem Grund vielleicht eher mit Nordlichtern, mit Naturbereichen also, die dem menschlichen Auge meist verborgen bleiben. Die natürliche Künstlichkeit oder künstliche Natur der Bildwelten, die Lergon mit seinen phthalogrünen Gemälden eröffnet, versetzt den Betrachter in einen emotionalen Zwiespalt von Faszination und Fremdheit. Die Vielfalt der Formen, die sich in diesen Gemälden zeigen, eröffnet ansatzweise immer wieder Anhaltspunkte für figurative Lesarten: Man glaubt zuweilen pflanzen- und tierhafte Gebilde zu erkennen, vielleicht Blütenkelche, Tentakel, Blätter von Schlingpflanzen oder Seetang oder auch Flügel und Beine von Tieren sowie hier und da sogar Andeutungen menschlicher Körper, scheitert jedoch beim Versuch, eine konsistente Bildlichkeit innerhalb eines Gemäldes zu etablieren. In der Betrachtung oszillieren die Motive stets zwischen fragmentarischer Figuration und der bloßen, im Farbmaterial bewahrten Spur des Malprozesses selbst. Es gehört zu den faszinierenden Aspekten dieser Malerei, dass man mit ihr als Betrachter zu keinem Ende kommt.

About Green

Peter Lodermeyer

"Green"—this is the short and sweet answer you would most likely receive if you asked visitors what paintings by Daniel Lergon looked like at his most recent exhibitions. That they are green really does describe them to a large degree, since they unfurl a profuse amount of green, perhaps excessively so, especially when you are looking at a larger number of these works next to one another at exhibitions. Their greenness establishes an overarching connection between the individual pictures—one that goes beyond their format differences and their distances on the walls and makes them appear as individual excerpts or insights into an entirely idiosyncratic image world. The fact that oil paint plays a predominant material role in these paintings presents an eye-opening new moment in Lergon's work. If we were also to characterize his earlier works in just a few concise words, in the case of Lergon's earlier paintings on retro-reflective canvases, we would probably first emphasize how they change as one gazes at them; when talking about the wall works using metal pigments we would cite the dull, dry material quality of the paint substances; and when referring to his paintings with acidified water on a metal ground, we would highlight the structures that result from these chemical processes. What the green paintings have in common both with the retro-reflective paintings and those carried out on metal grounds is that here, too, the painting ground plays an important role, as is indicated by the title *Unter Grün* (Under the Green). In the earlier paintings, the influence of the background—the retro-reflective canvas or the metals—determined the light and color effects, which had been produced physically or chemically. With the green paintings, the painting ground chosen serves as a kind of reflector determining the degree to which the varying density of the applied paint substance is revealed.

Subsequent to Lergon's study of unusual materials and surfaces, it is paint as color that is central to the green paintings the artist has been creating since the end of 2015—something he demonstrates using a classic painterly medium: oil on canvas. It initially seems that, using a traditional manner of painting, the artist simply wished to apply and test the experience he has gathered from many years of experimenting with new painting means and picture carriers. But as a matter of fact, with his green paintings, he also probes oil paint as a material substance and certainly not just as mere color; the color green is for him both color and paint substance—something we only notice at a second, closer, glance. The gradations of color shades and the nuances of brightness, which reveal astonishing effects in these paintings, result directly from the material characteristics obtained through the exclusive use of a single oil color: phthalo green. This specific green is emphasized by means of the varying density of its application, whereby its effect is very dependent on whether it has been applied to a white or a neon-yellow ground.

We as viewers find it hard to believe that there is really only one single color at work in these paintings. Regardless of how they look initially, the darkest parts are in no way black, but rather a deep, velvety dark green. One of the material characteristics of phthalo green is that, depending on the manner and thickness of its application, it produces an unusually broad spectrum of brightness gradations, ranging from the aforementioned near-black when it is applied as impasto to a poisonously glowing, blue-tinged green hue when it has been heavily thinned. Lergon brings out the possibilities and various color shades of the painting material, "opening up" the color, as it were, by spreading out its wealth of nuances. Since Lergon completely exhausts the spectrum of brightness nuances with the rich internal differentiation of his motifs, the thought would hardly occur to us to refer to these works as "monochrome paintings." Instead, their wealth of nuances makes them appear "multi-monochrome," to borrow this term from the exhibition title *Multimono* (Galerie Christian Lethert, Cologne, 2016). Moreover, these pieces work with the elementary principle of Gestalt psychology, something otherwise carefully avoided in monochrome painting: the opposite of figure and ground. The diversity of the brightness values in Lergon's paintings and the illusionistic effects resulting from them call to mind more the traditional notion of chiaroscuro than the modern term monochromy. It is certainly tempting to regard Lergon's green paintings as a new interpretation of the light/dark painting in the way it was prevalent in the art of the Baroque era—we need only think of Caravaggio or Rembrandt. Here, the modeling of the motifs with light and shadows has been entirely shifted to the different green tones, and enhanced even more where Lergon uses a neon-yellow grounding instead of white. By means of this, the paintings' effect of light and depth is vastly intensified. The yellow is not employed as a second color, but as a light-filled background, which pervades the green color, pushing it further into the spectrum of yellow, and thus, heightening its radiance. Only on the narrow sides of the painting is the yellow able to unfold itself as such and, due to the reflection of the light from the surrounding environment, be in a position to conjure up a radiant aura on the walls around the paintings.

The modeling of the picture motifs—if indeed it is even possible to speak of "motifs"—comes about by using various instruments for applying and distributing the paint. Depending on whether or not and, if so, how Lergon applies the paint with a narrow brush, uses a sponge, or smears or removes from the surface again with scrapers and palette knives, clear differences emerge in the brightness and texture causing a confusing illusion of depth and spatiality—a spatiality, which is nevertheless not homogeneous, but turns out to be inconsistent, keeping the eye busy (and at the same time overstraining it) with the forming of the gestalt structure, that is to say with the attempt to bring what has been seen into a harmonious spatial order. Since Lergon always adds to these "motifs" sufficient unstructured surfaces applied homogeneously with the roller, they appear as "figures" before their respective background. We can distinguish between four different picture types, depending upon whether the work has been grounded in white or in neon yellow and whether the picture background has been executed as light or dark, which is to say: whether the phthalo green has been painted on very thickly or very thinly. Against the dark backgrounds, the "figures" stand out brightly, virtually suffused with light. In cases where the background green has only been applied thinly to a white ground, the background surface shines in turquoise green, and when applied to a vibrantly yellow ground, it appears more as a grass-green, causing the darker motifs to stand out as being all the more plastically modeled. In such cases, it becomes immediately clear just how much the appearance of the work depends upon the grounding and the brightness of the background.

Green is a color we almost inevitably associate with plants, nature, and the landscape. But the phthalo green Lergon uses seems oddly cold, introducing into the notion of nature a certain alienness, an emotional dissonance, that is difficult to describe in words. The reason for this is no doubt due to the fact that phthalo green is artificially produced as a pigment, namely from copper phthalocyanine. It was developed by the chemical industry, and has only been in production since 1938. If we take a look at the complex formula of the chemical structure, we see that at the center of each molecule there is a copper atom, which is surrounded by rings of sodium and chloride. Thus, the color material with its copper component is also chemically related to Lergon's earlier works on a copper ground.

The sheer presence of the strange coloration of the phthalo green invariably conjures up certain concrete notions on the part of the viewer. For example, we might associate the works on a white ground with underwater worlds, and those on a neon-yellow ground perhaps more with the northern lights, and thus with realms of nature that are mostly hidden from the human eye. The natural artificiality or artificial nature of these image worlds that Lergon opens up with his phthalo green paintings brings viewers into an emotional conflict between fascination and alienation. The multitude of forms revealed in these paintings gives continuous cues for figurative interpretation. At times we think we can discern plant and animal figurations, perhaps calyxes, tentacles, leaves of creeping vines, or seaweed or maybe also wings and legs of animals and, here and there, even indications of human bodies, but ultimately such attempts fail to establish a consistent pictorial quality within the individual painting. While viewing, the motifs always oscillate between fragmentary figuration and the mere trace of the painting process recorded in the painting substance. One of the fascinating aspects about these paintings is that as viewers we come to no end.

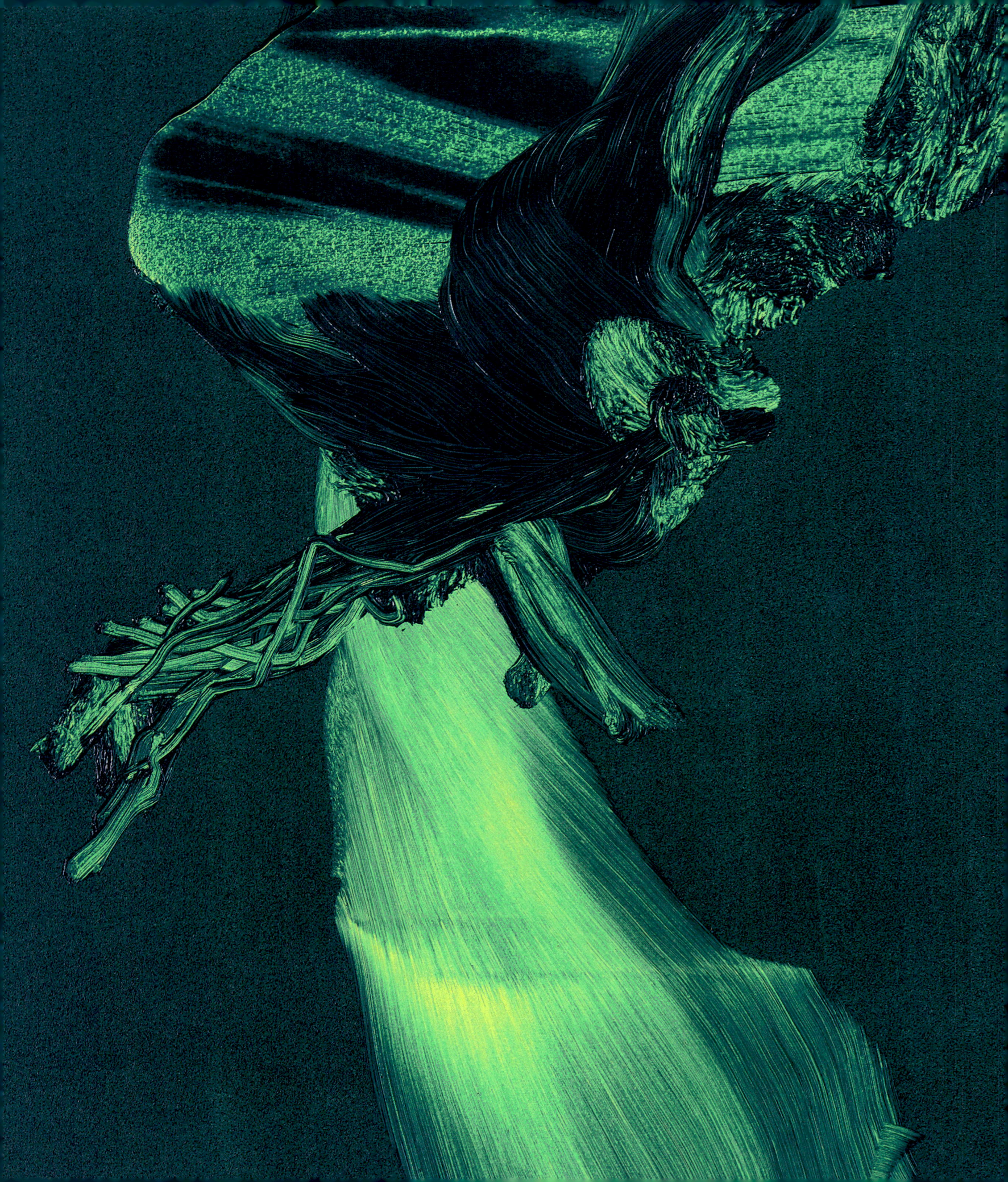

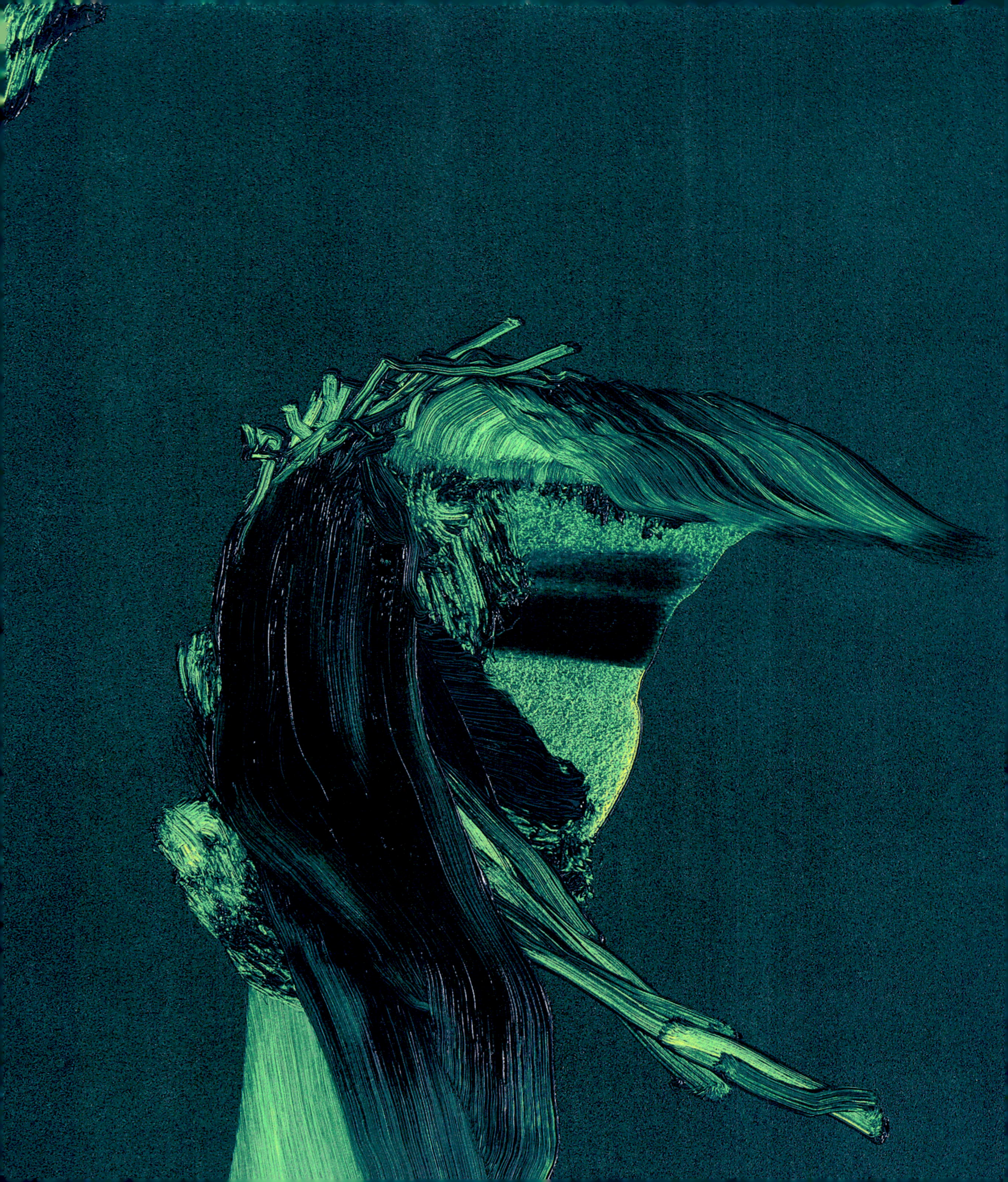

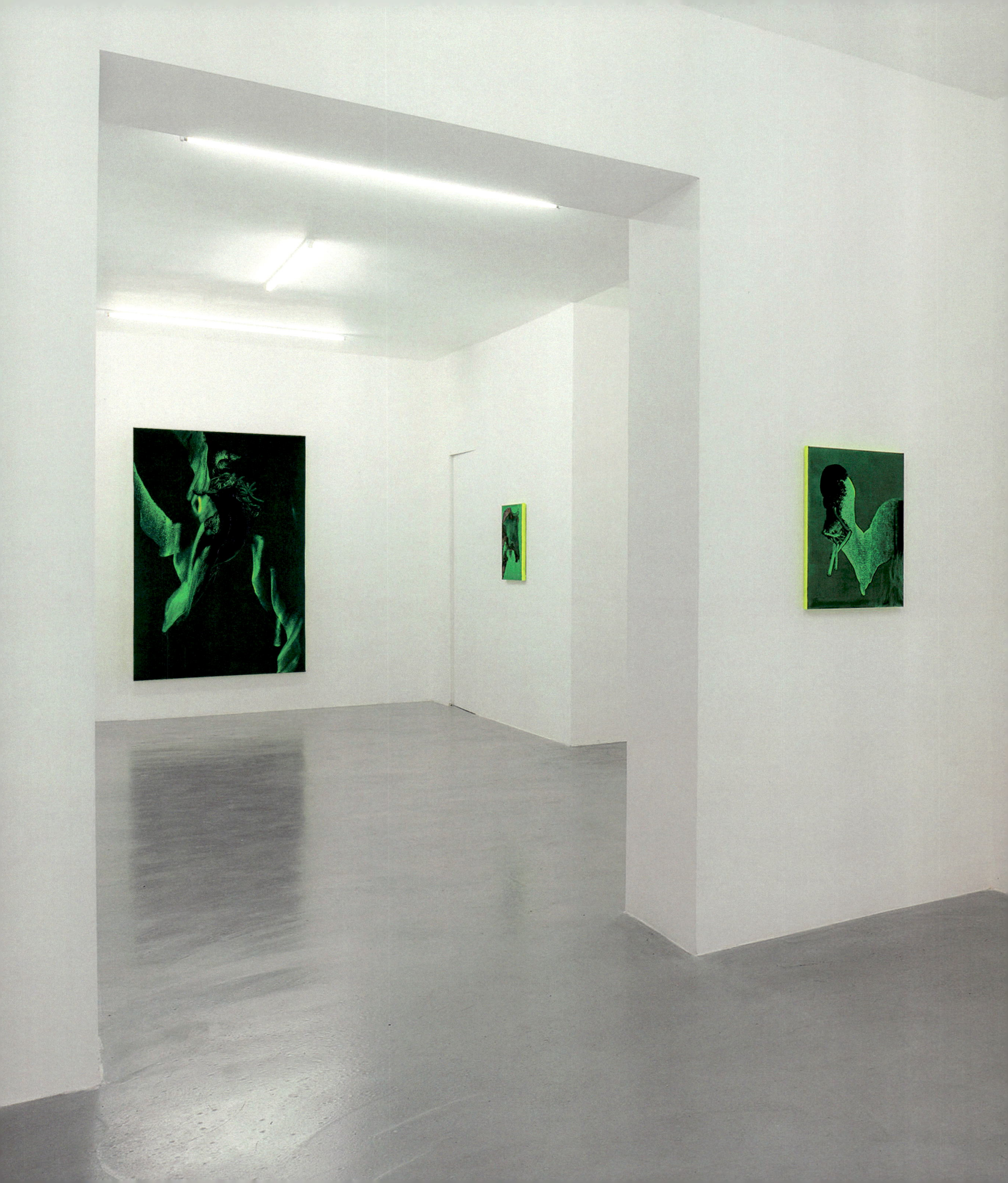

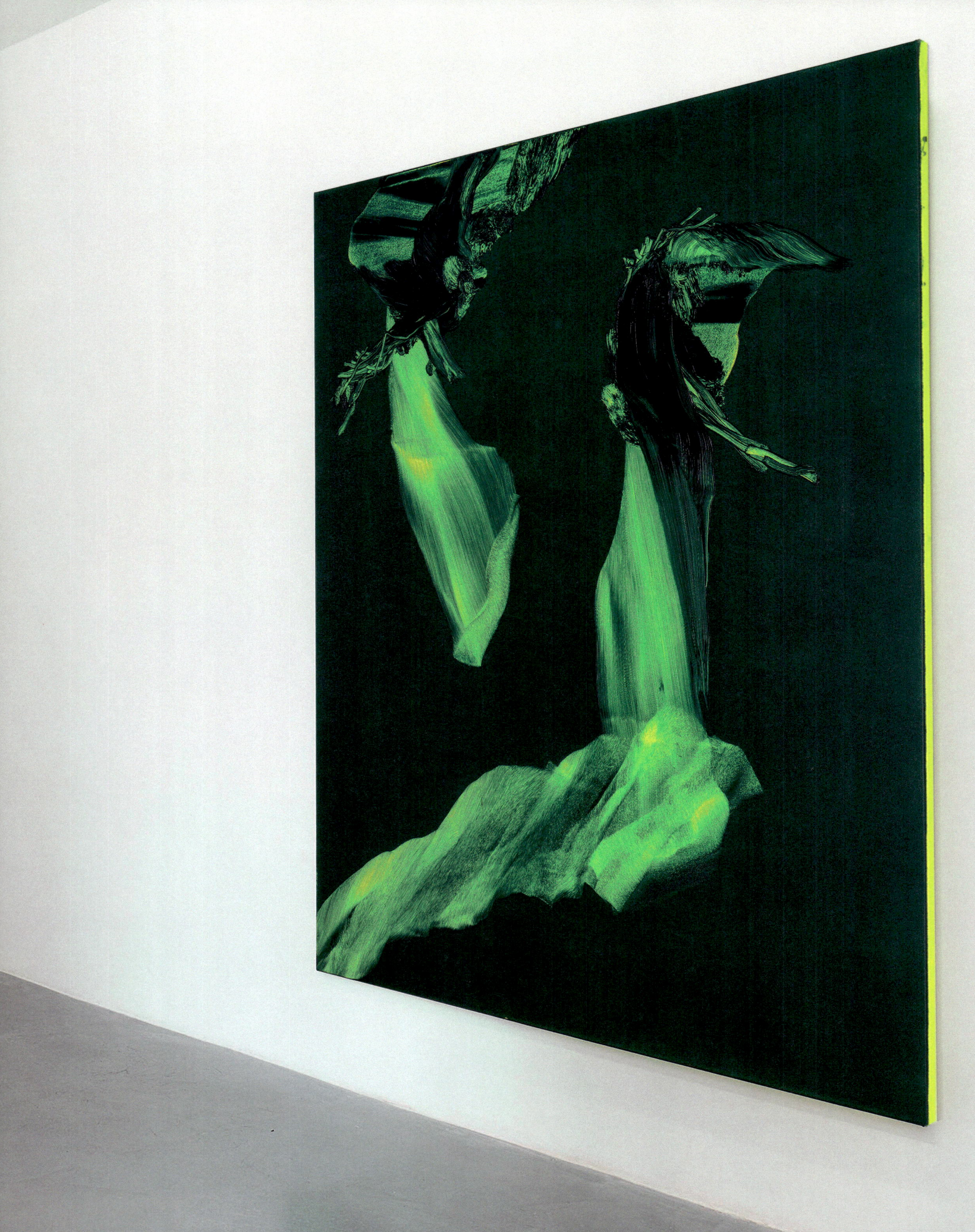

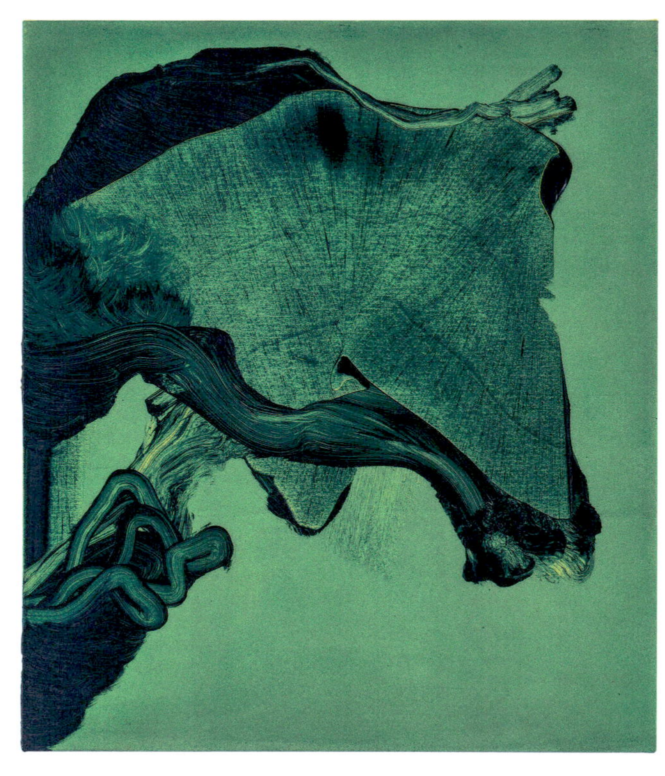

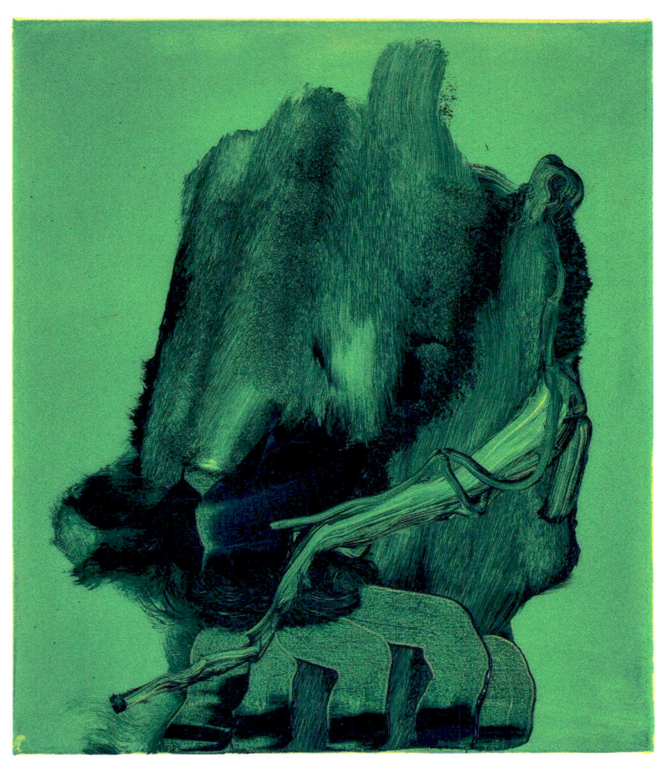

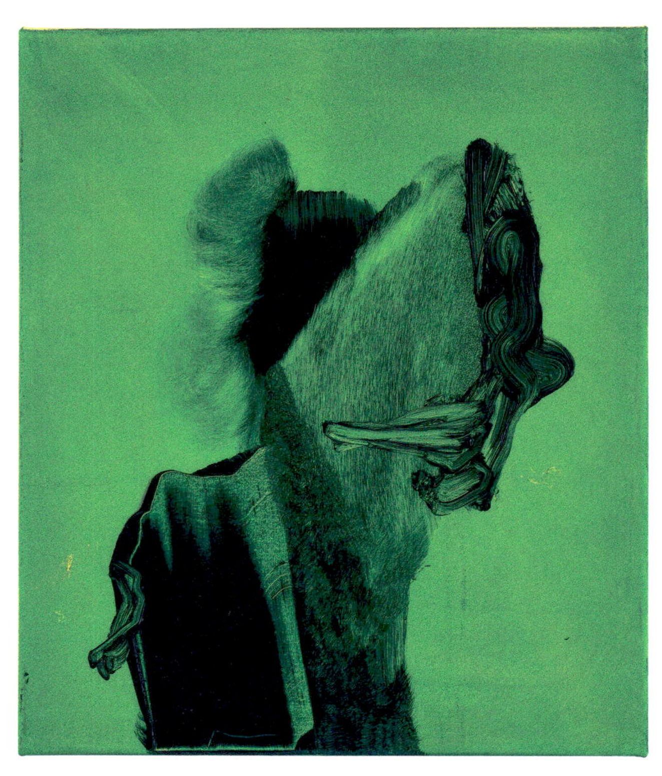

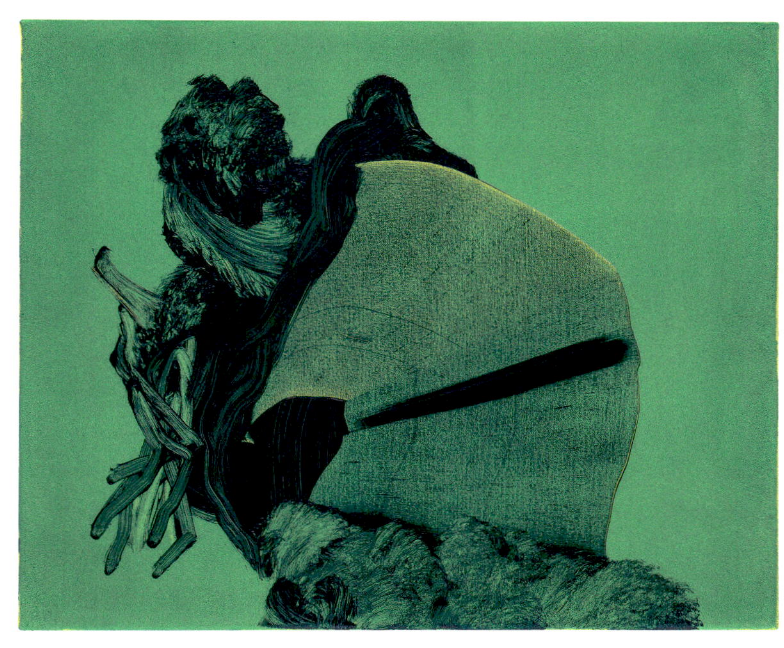

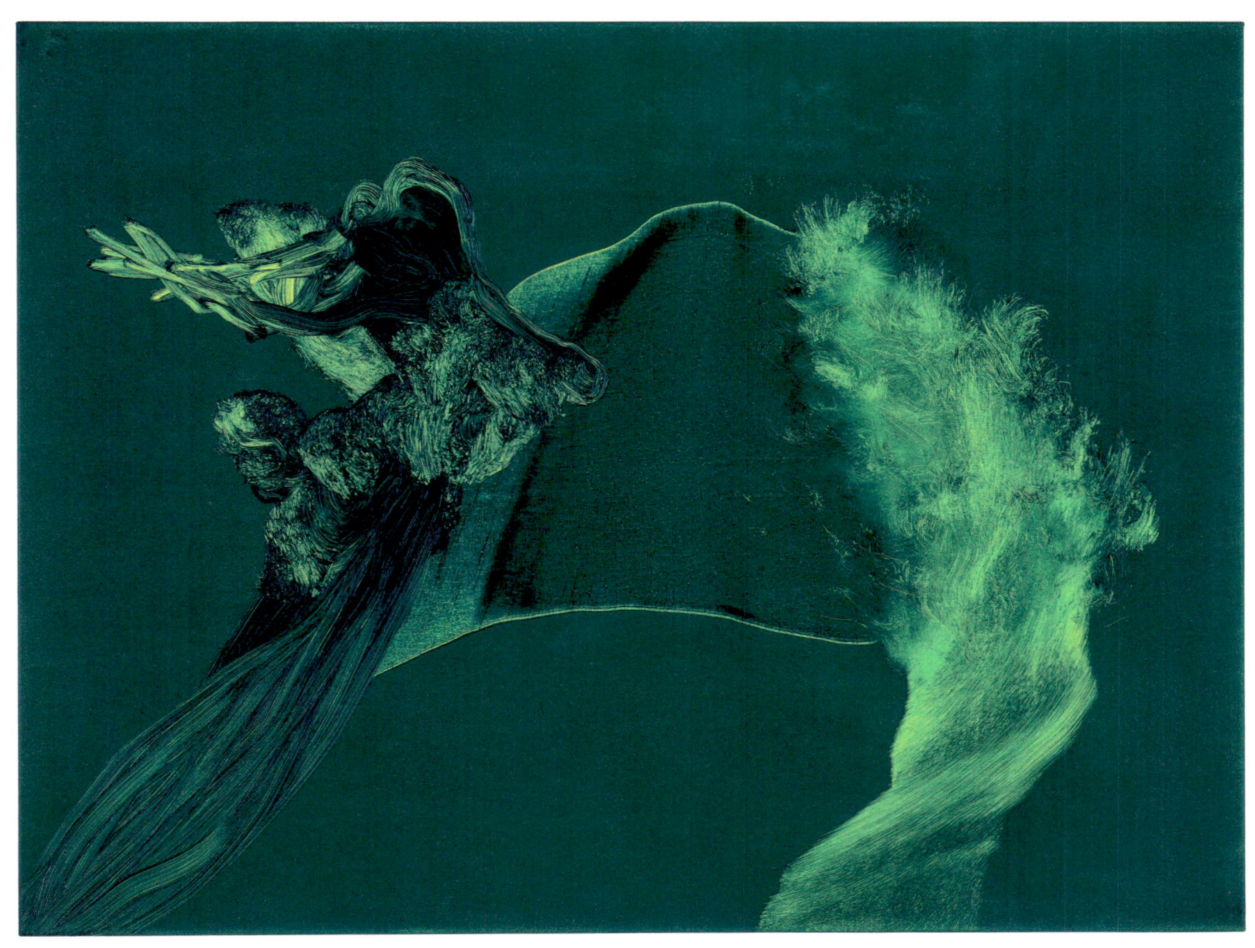

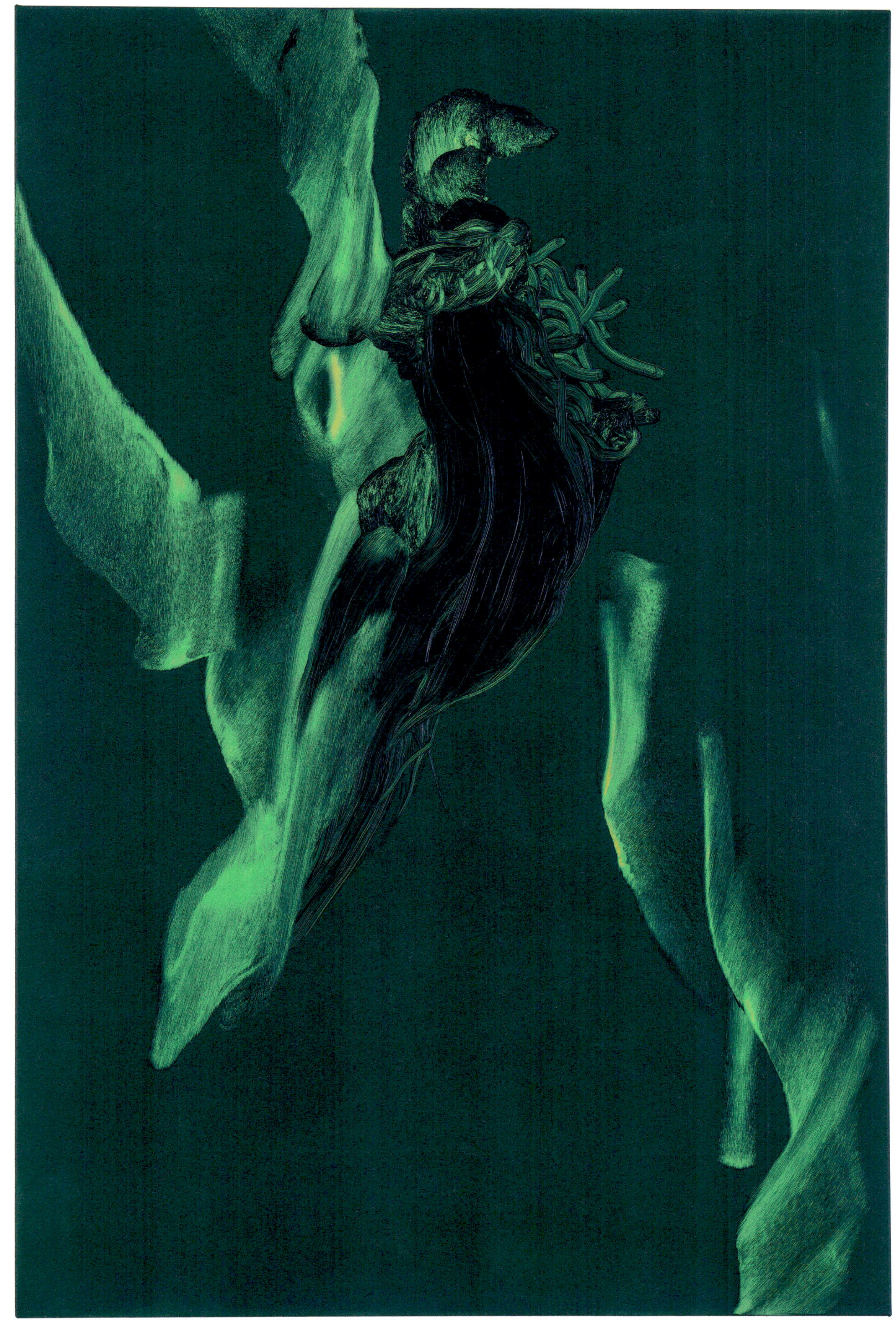

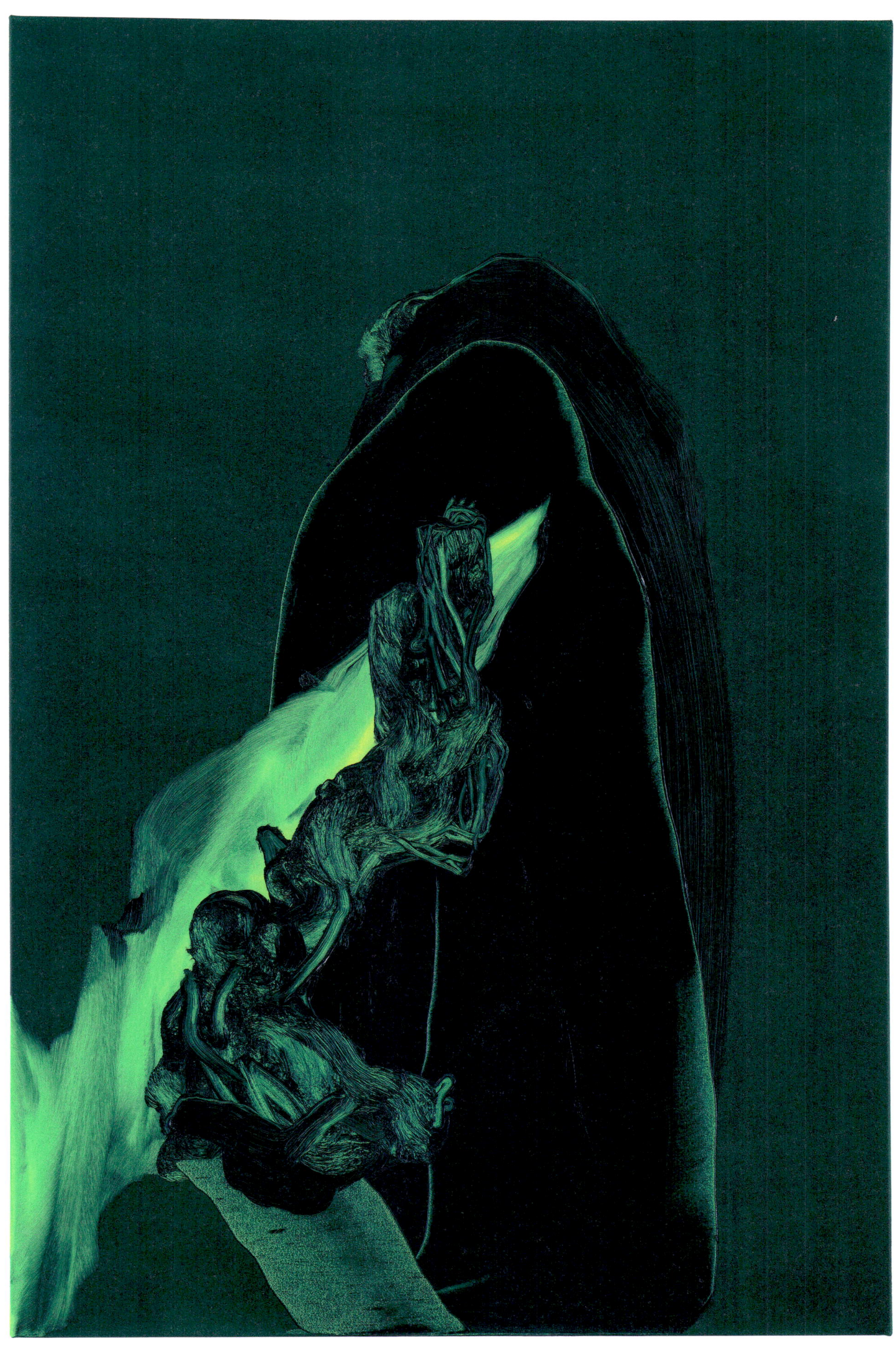

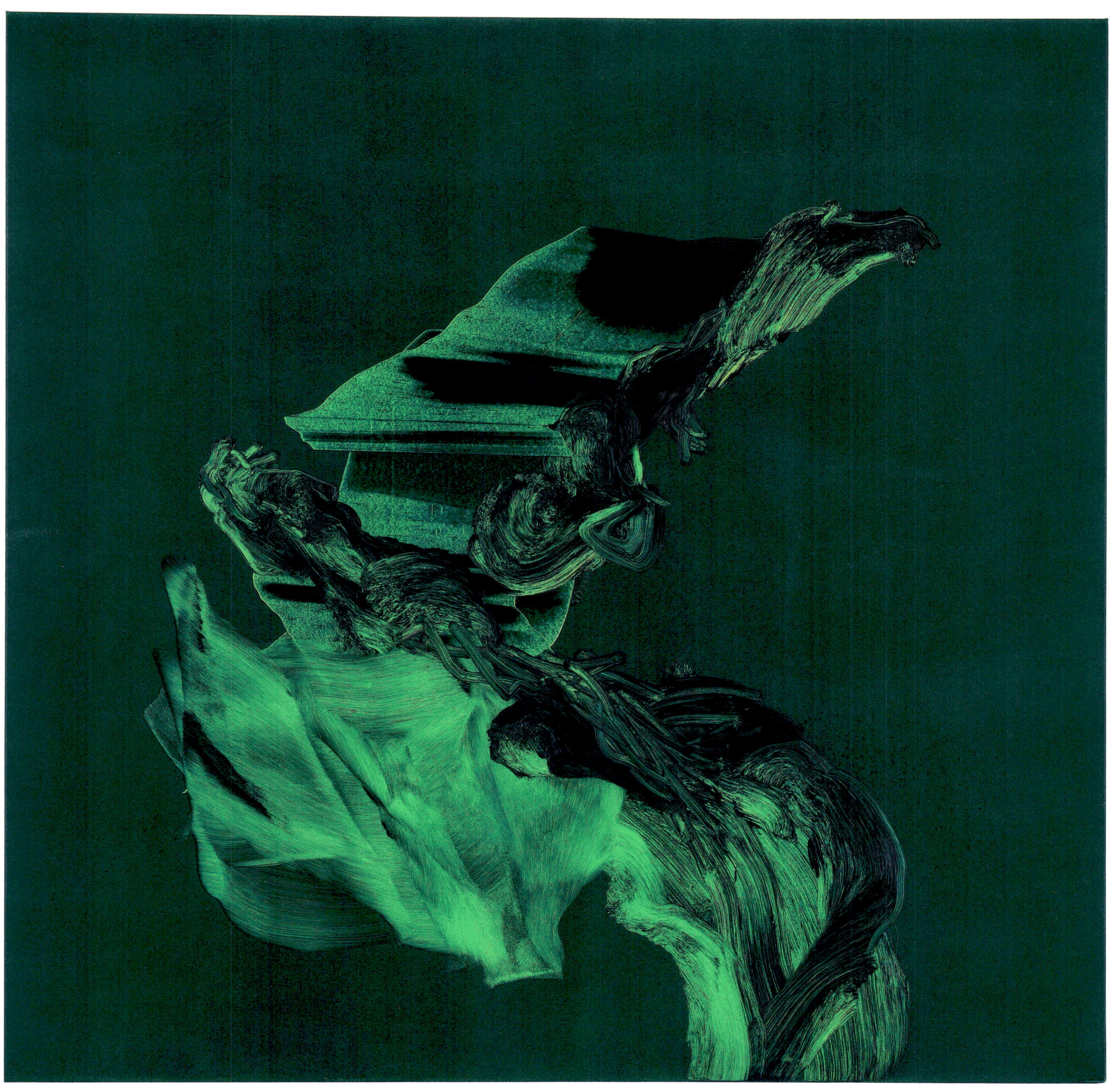

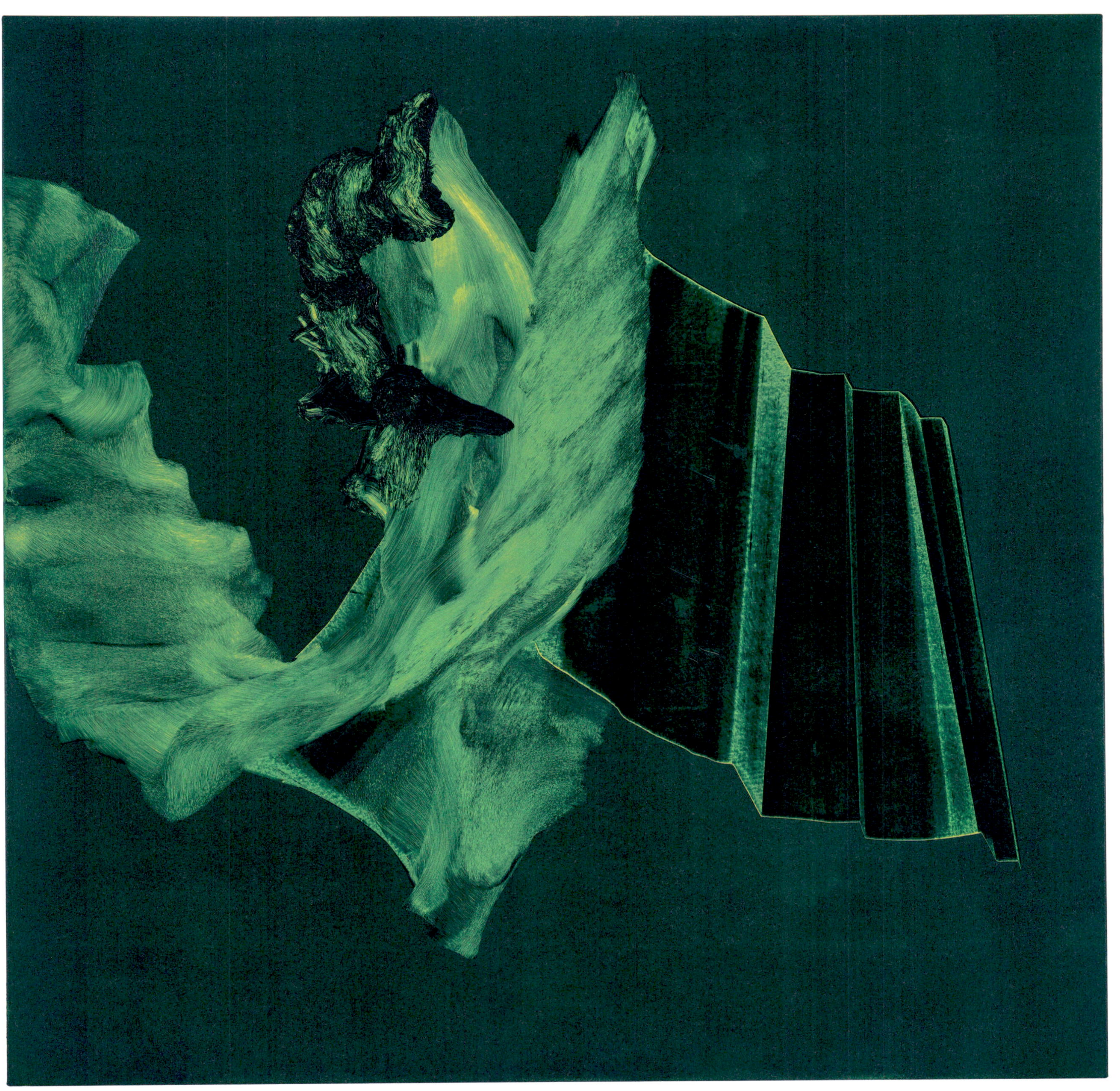

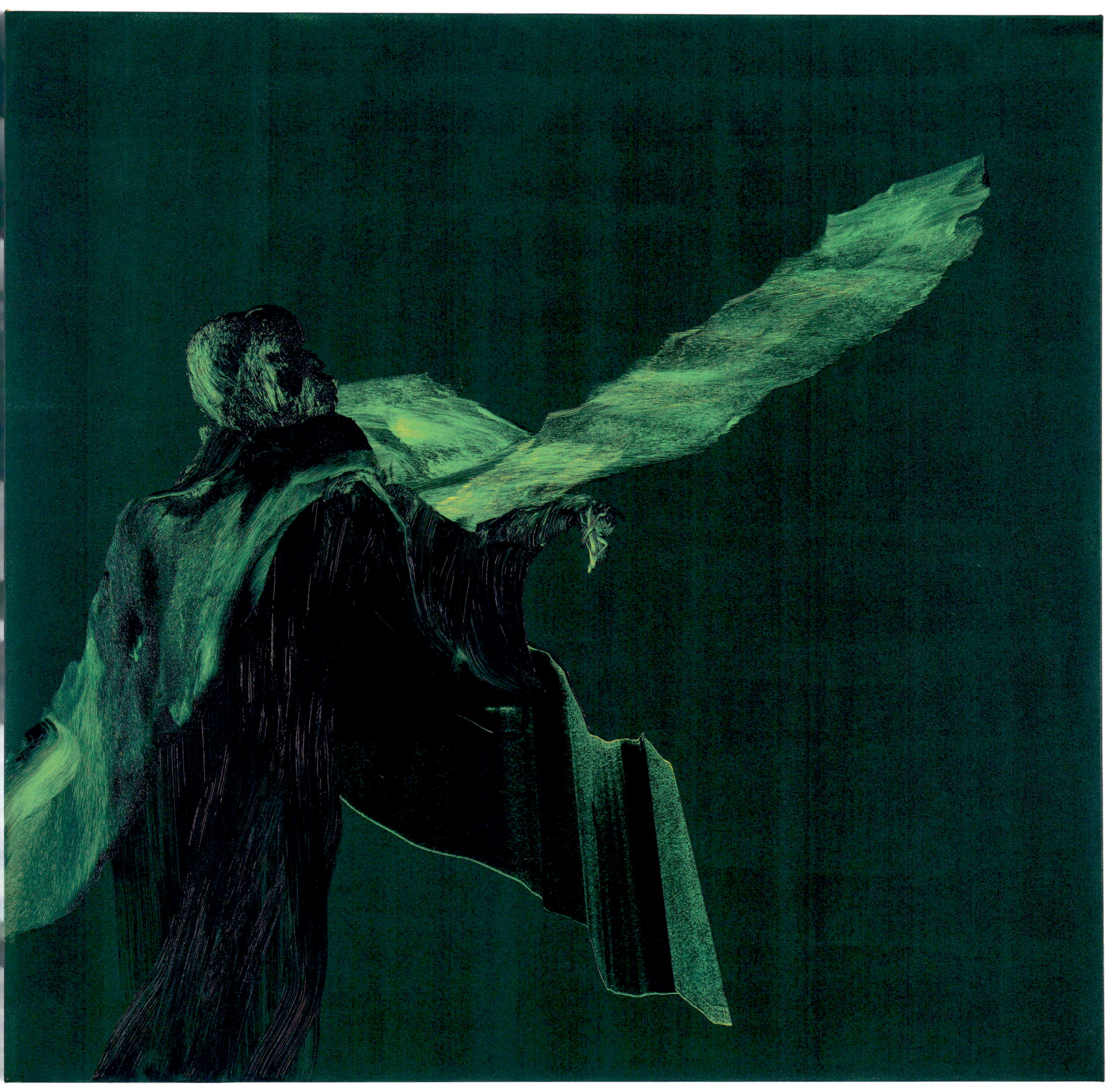

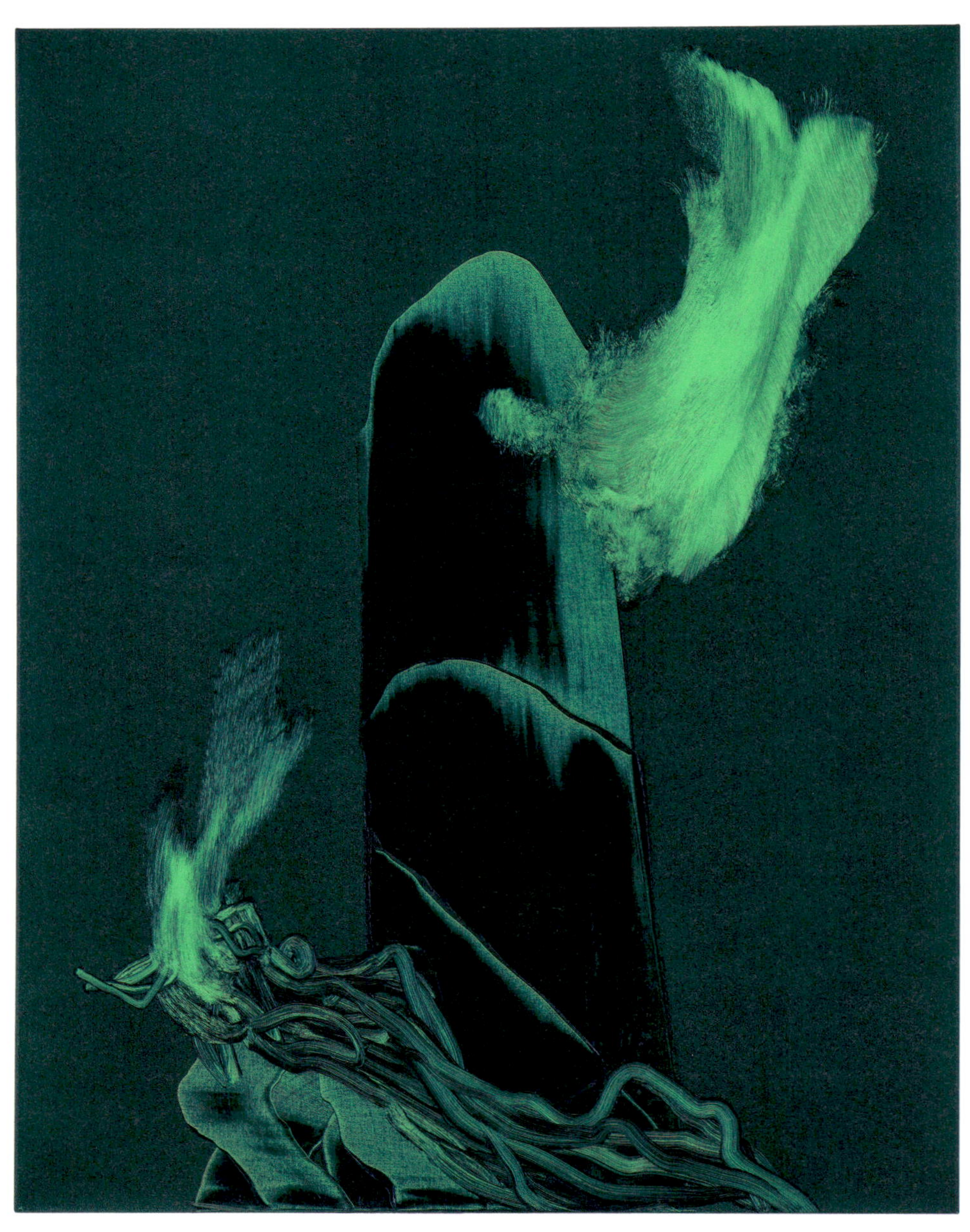

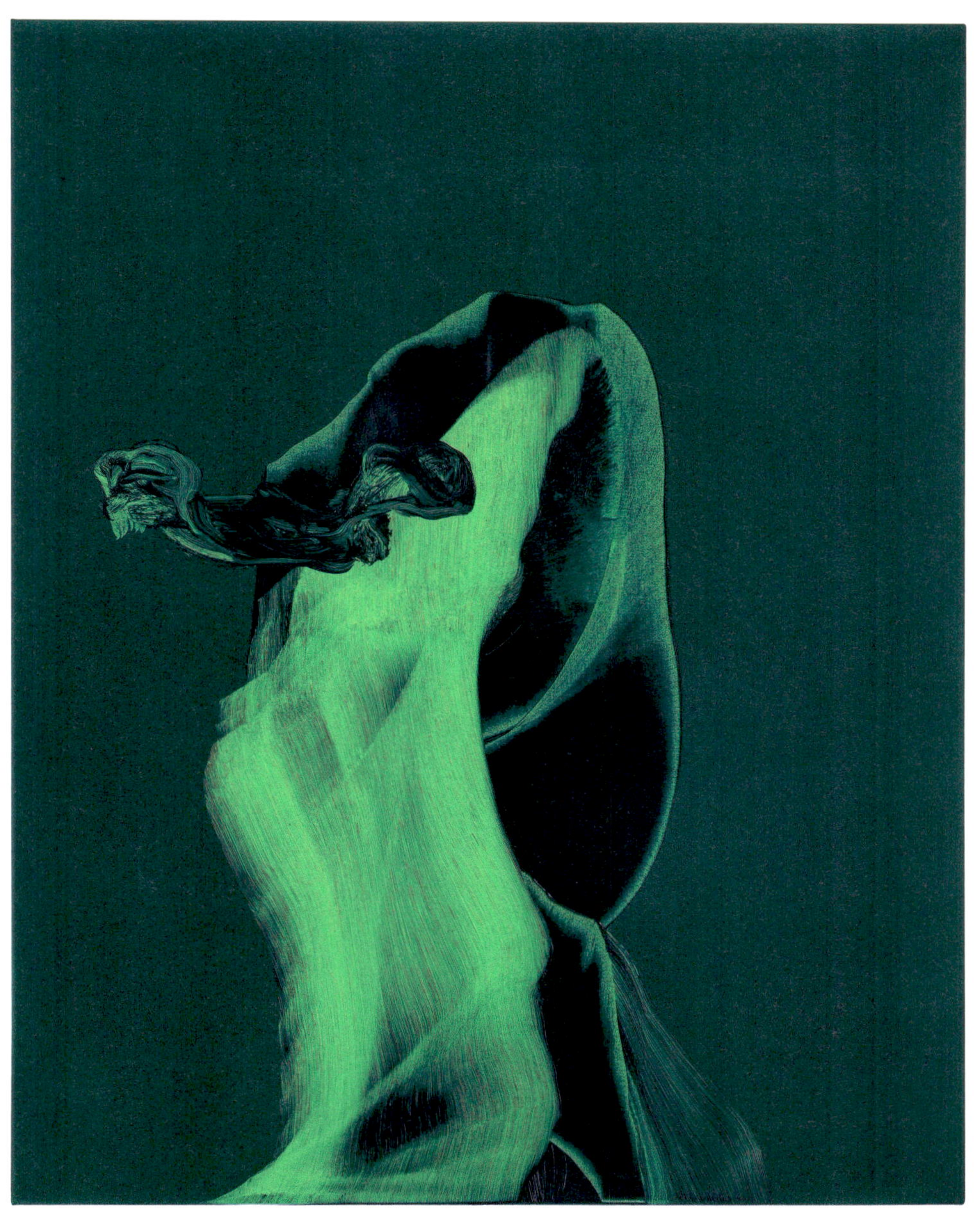

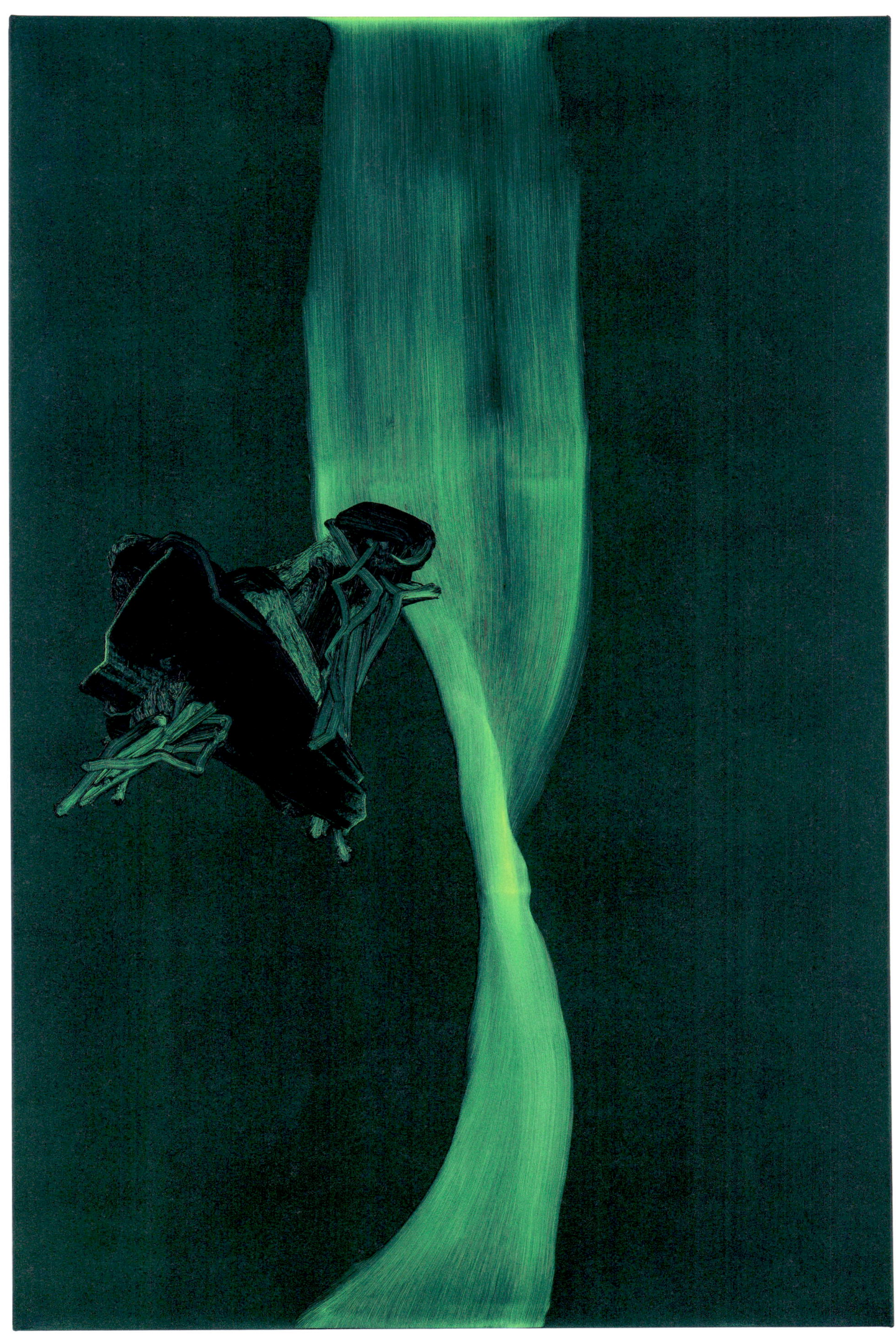

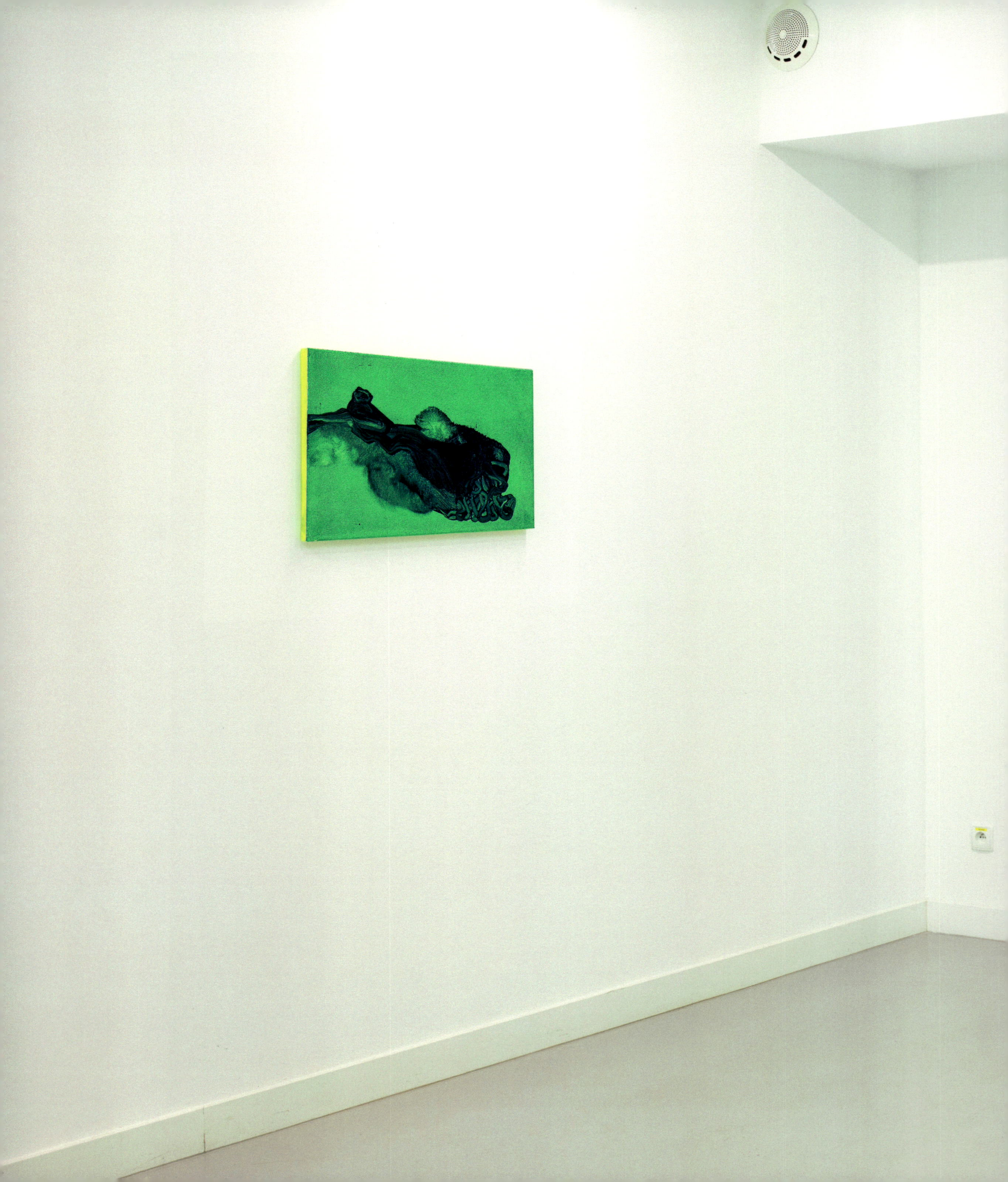

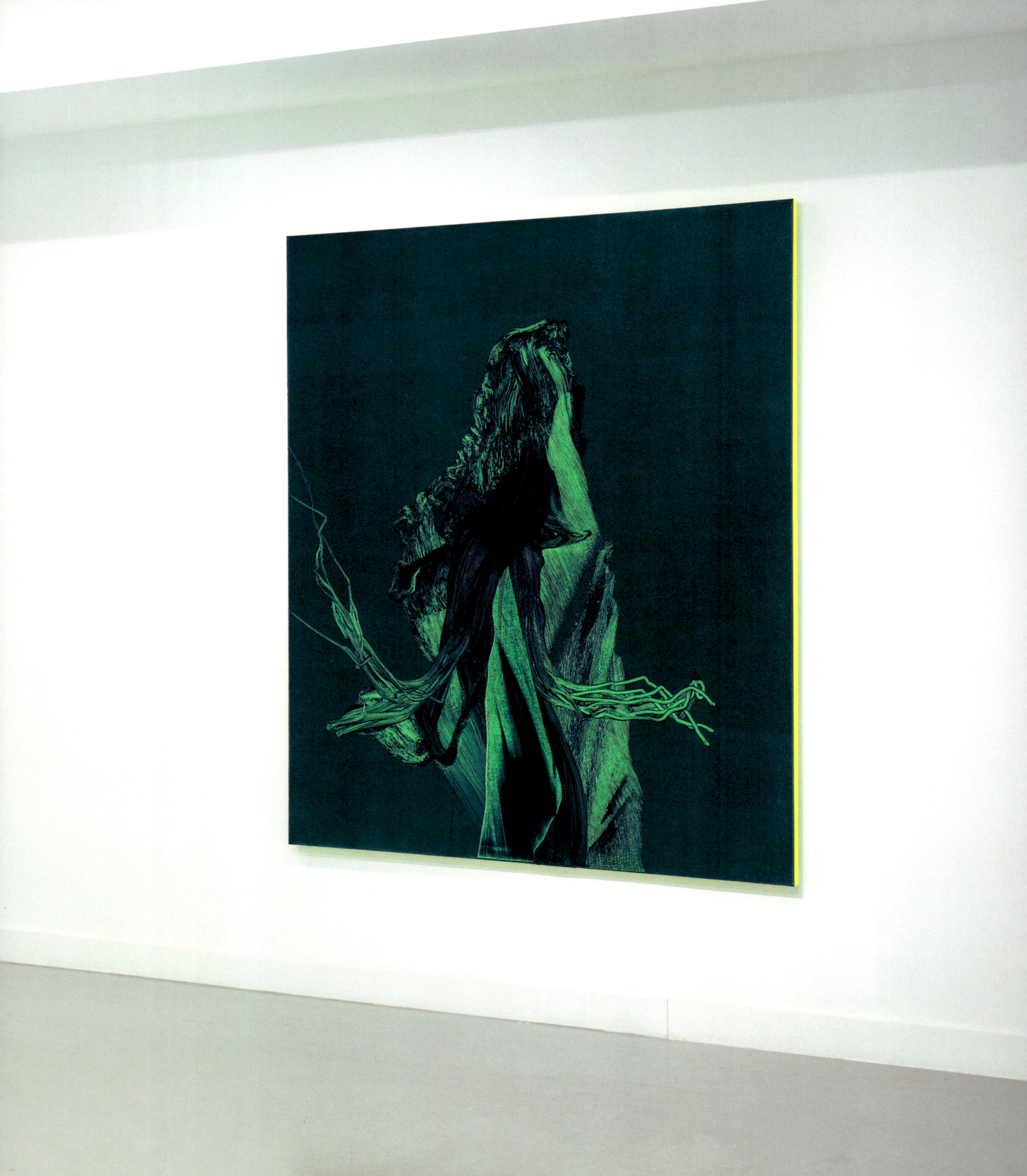

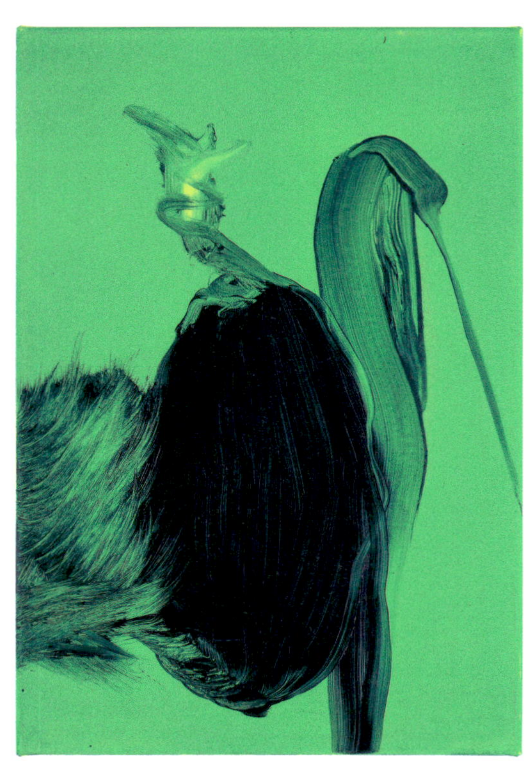

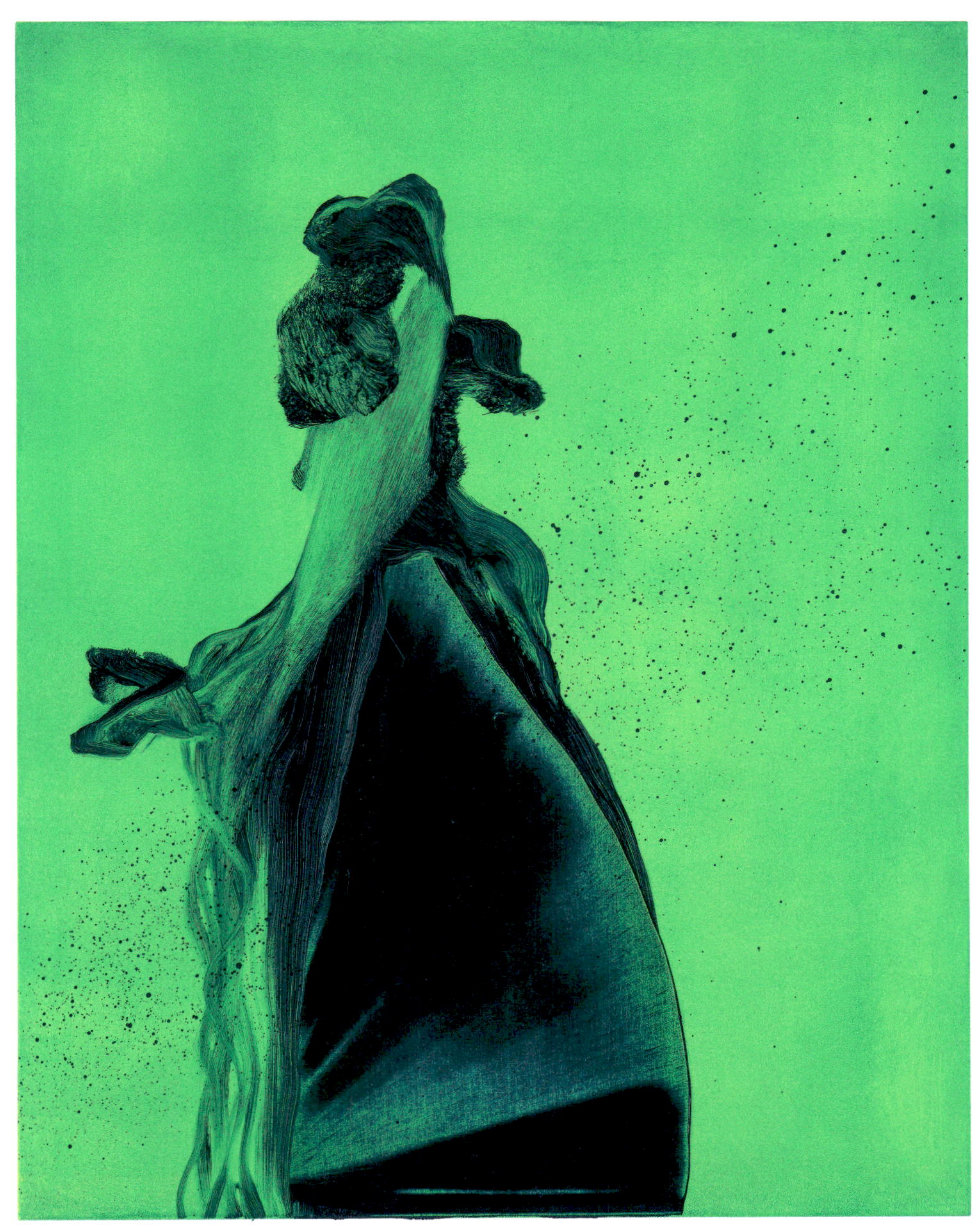

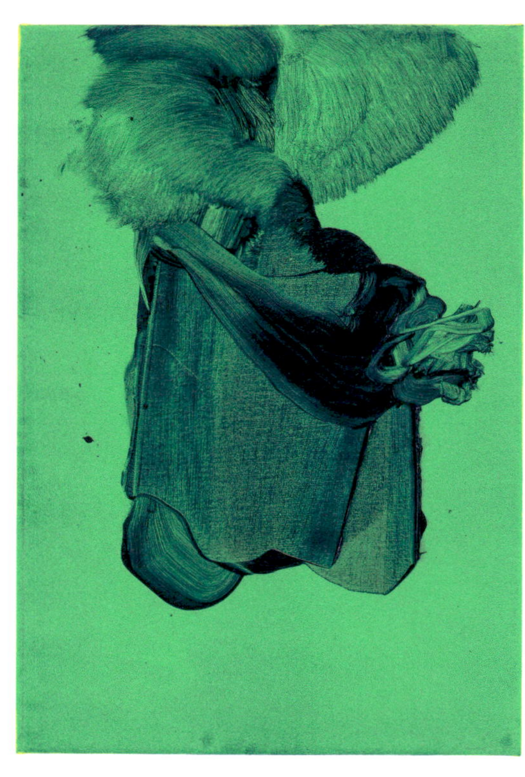

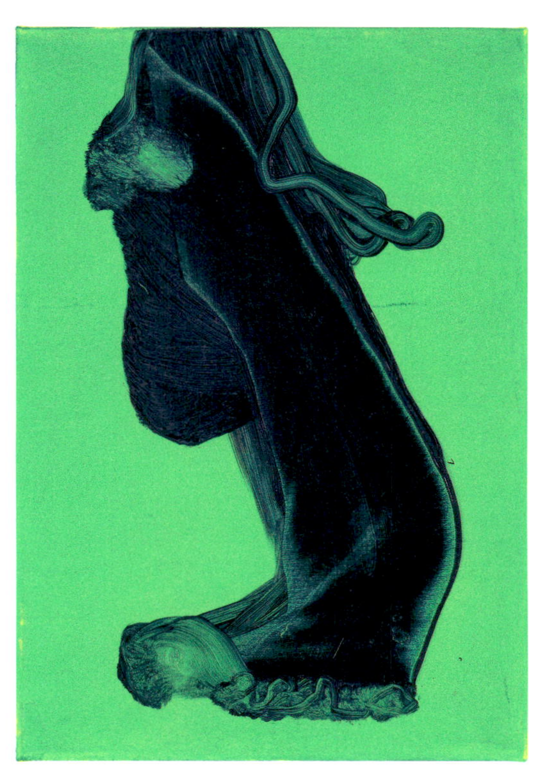

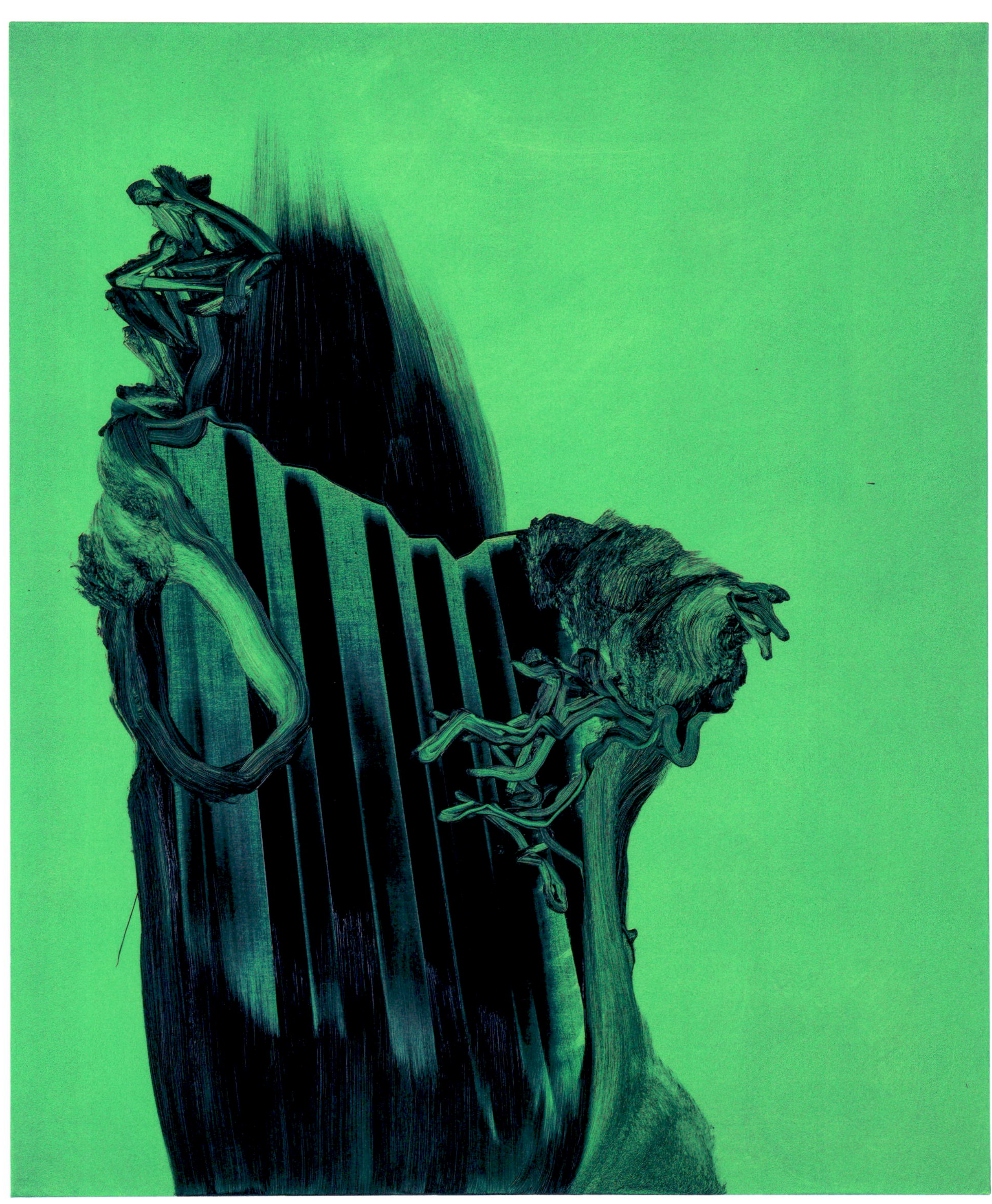

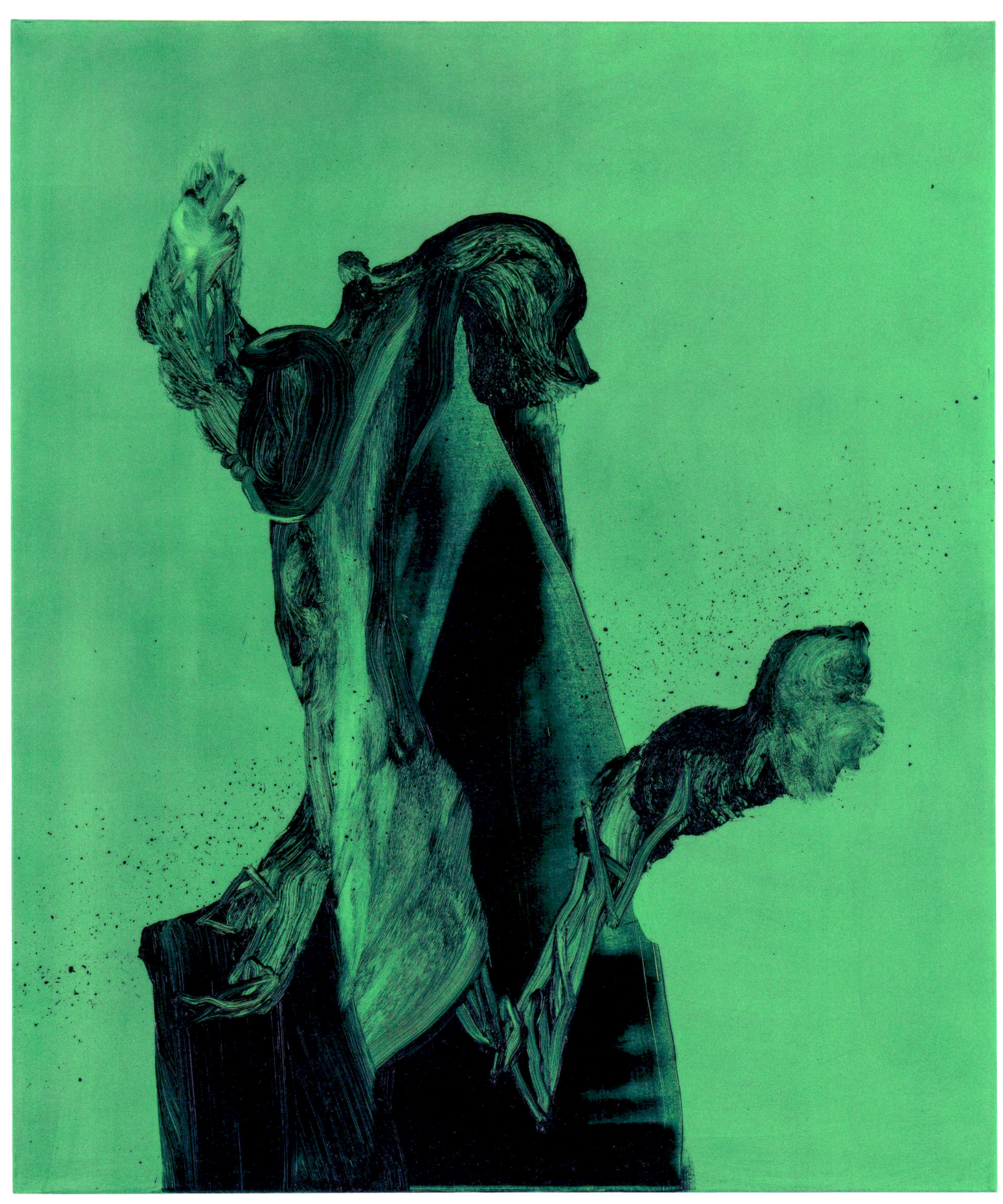

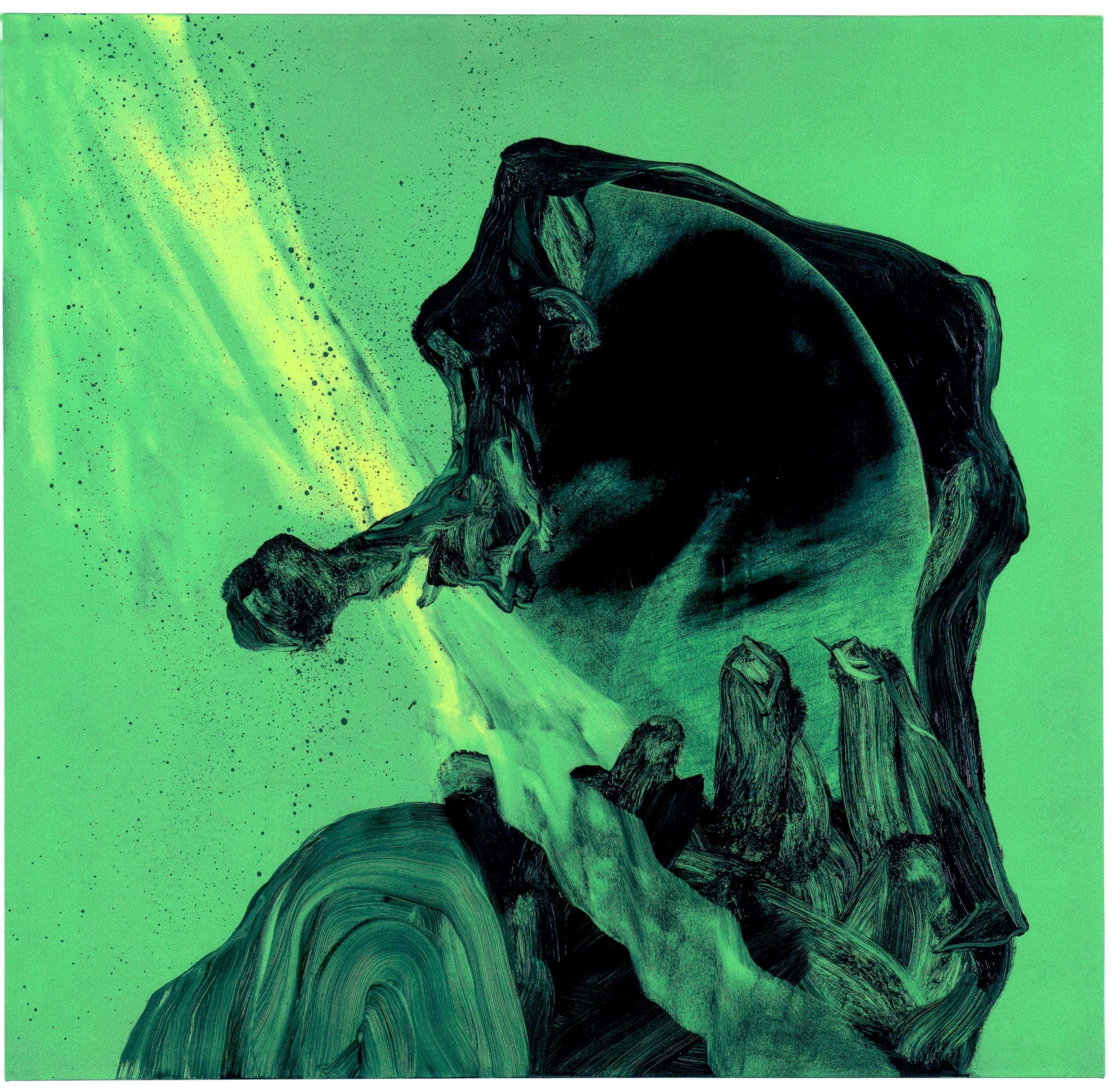

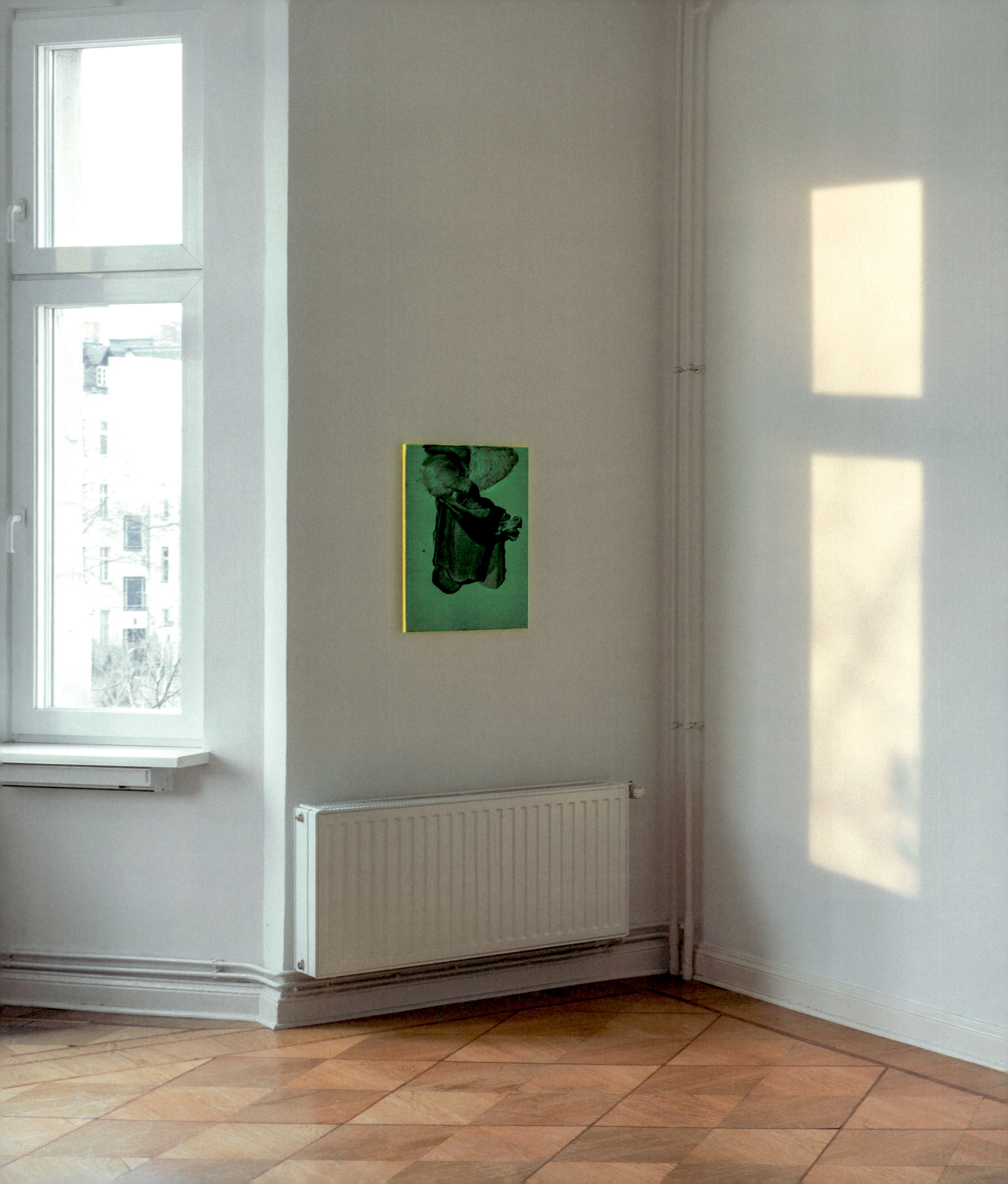

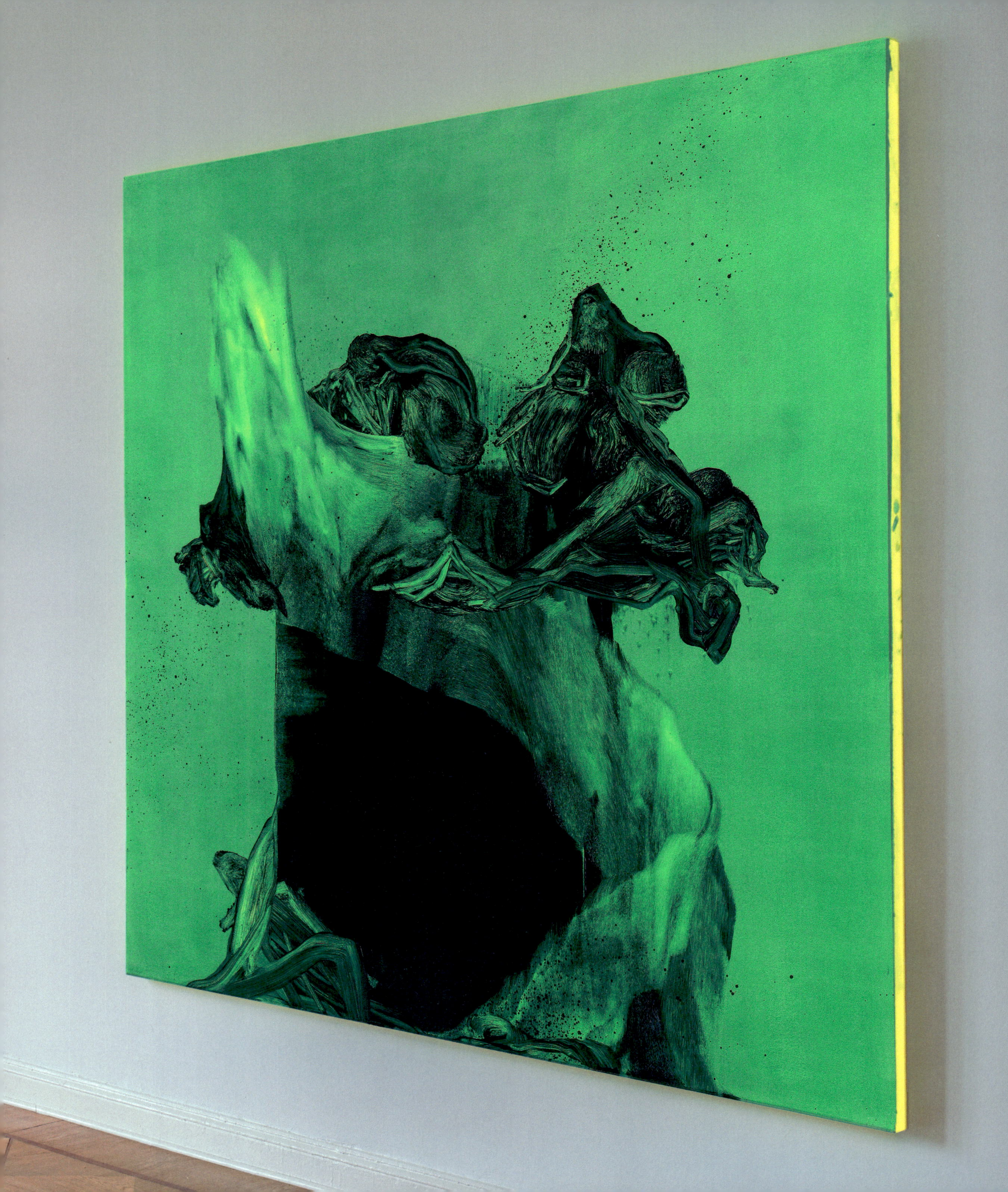

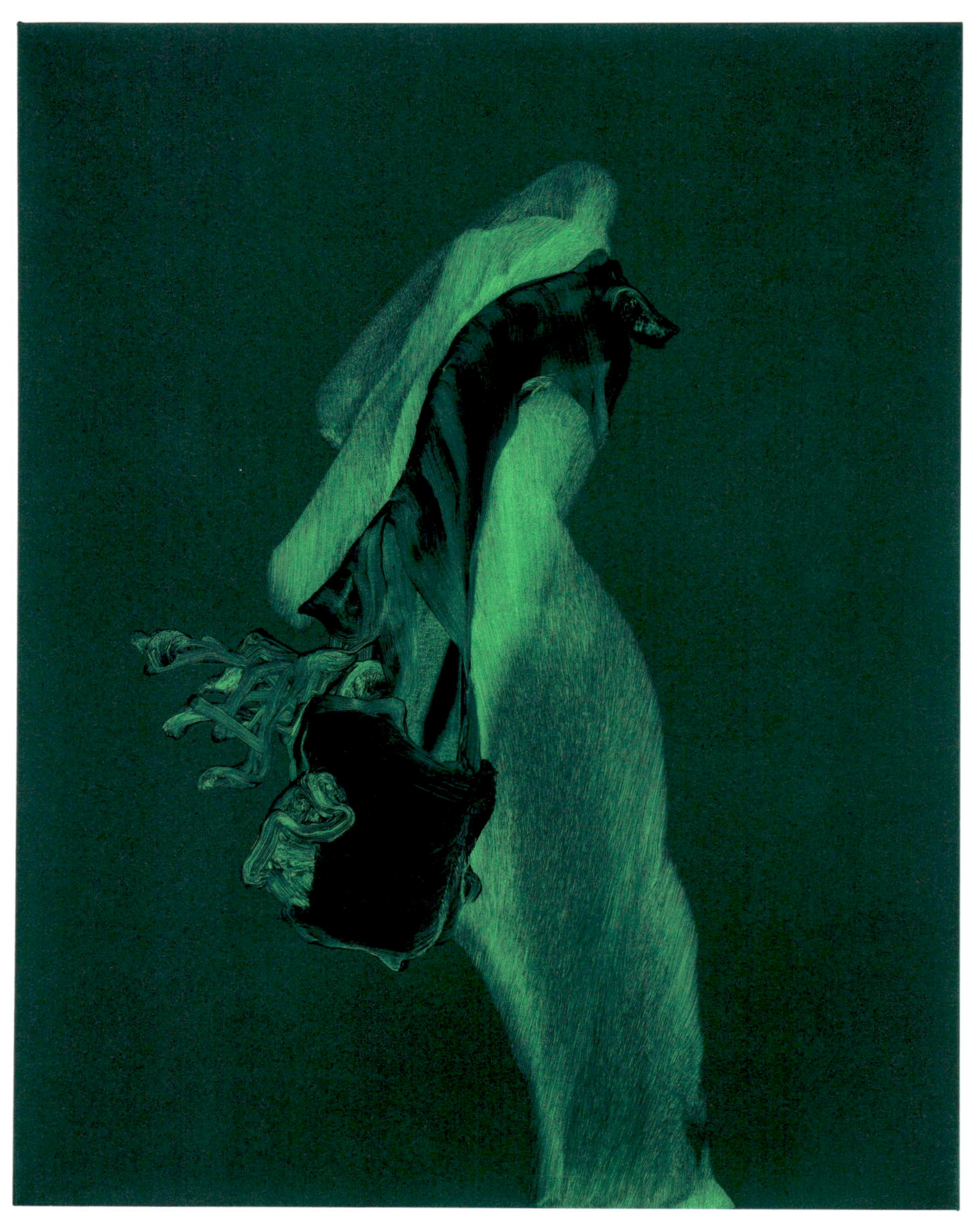

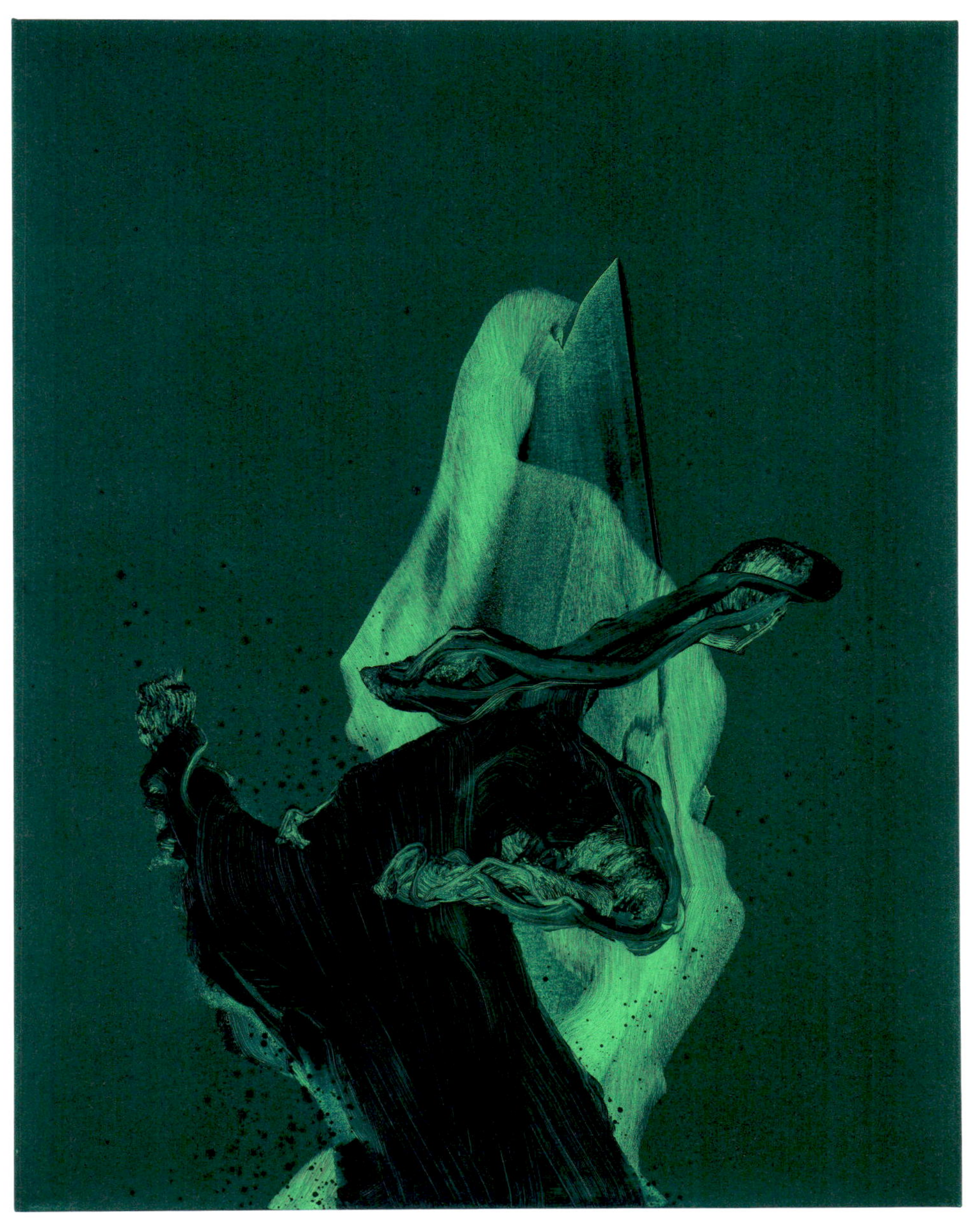

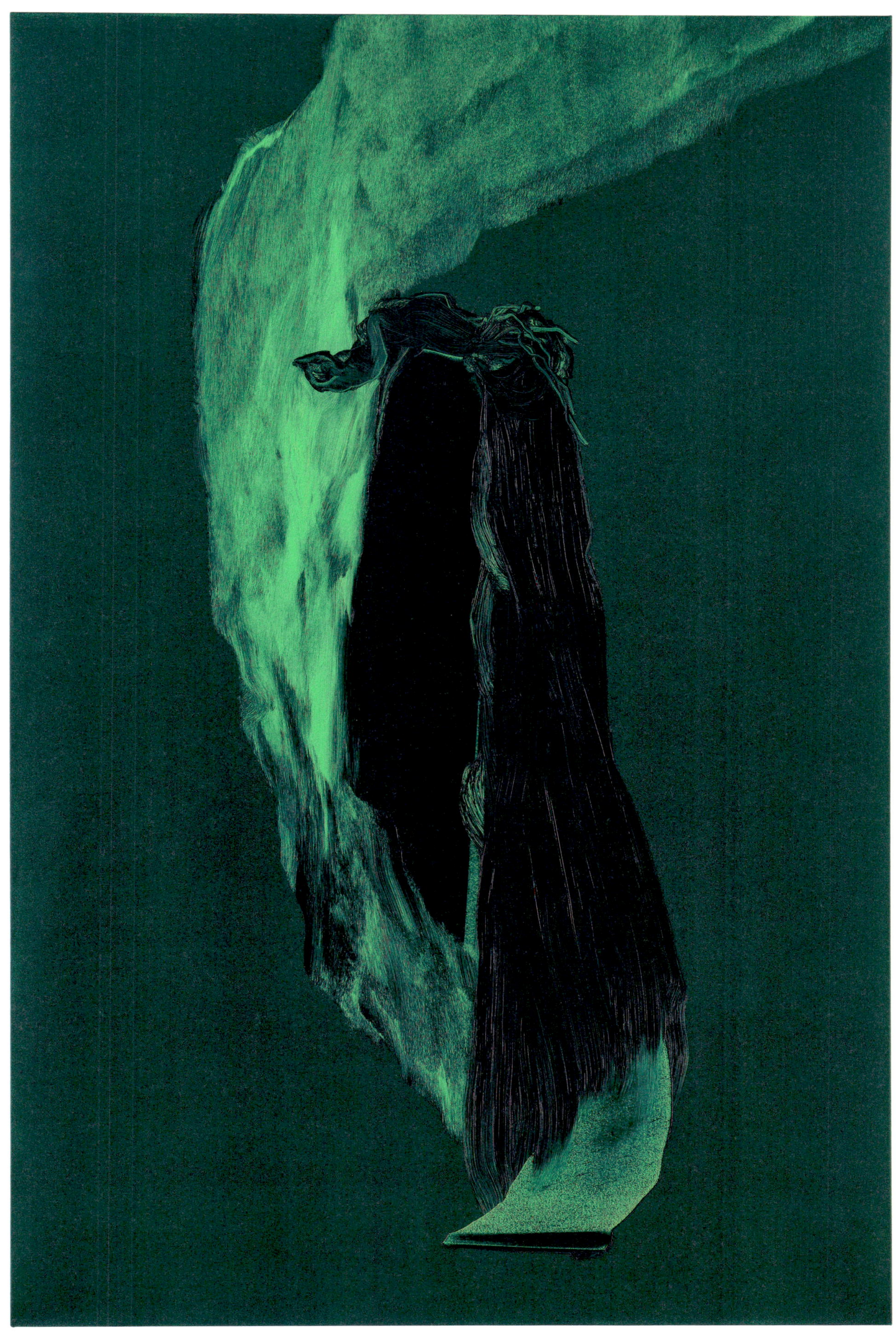

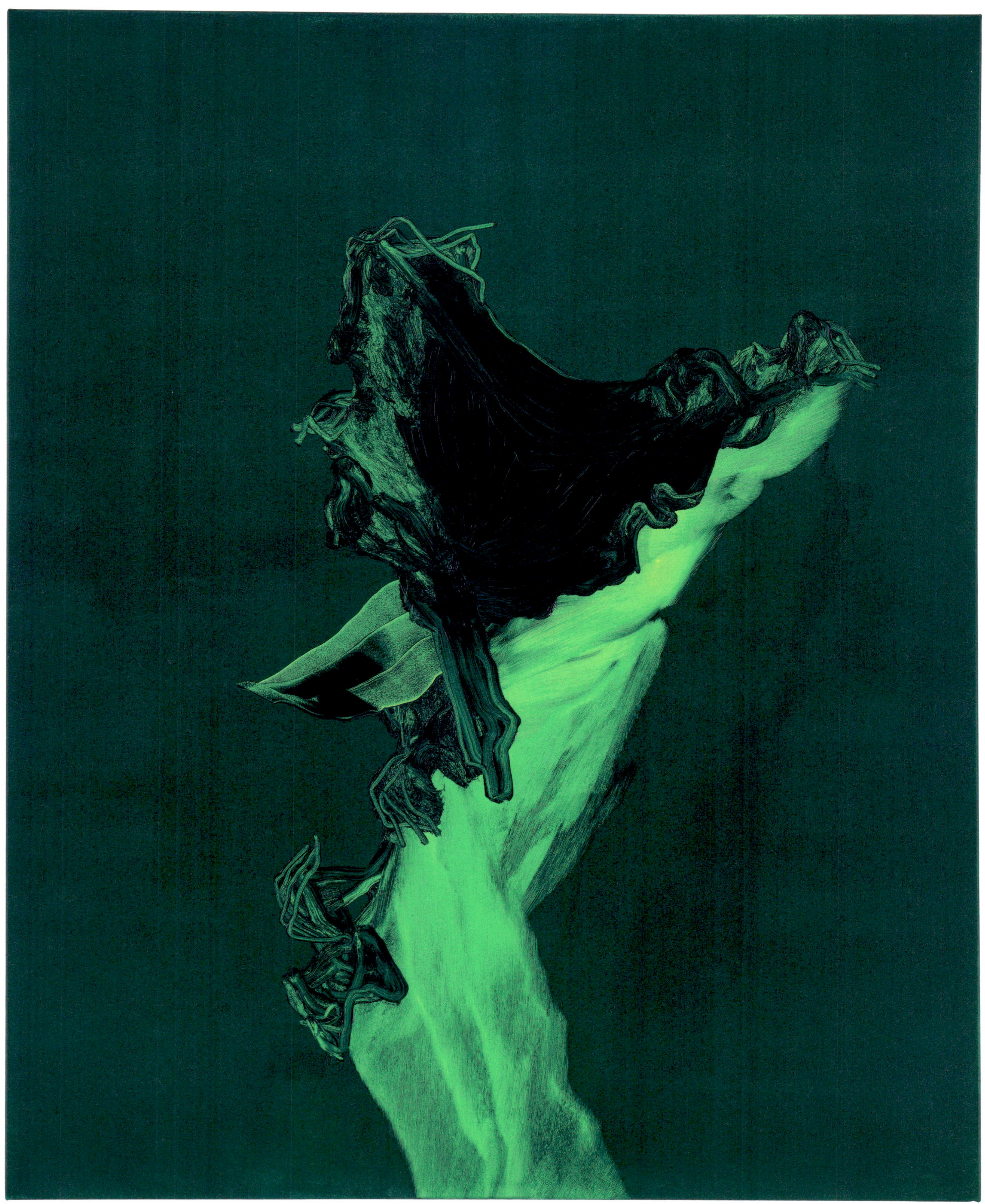

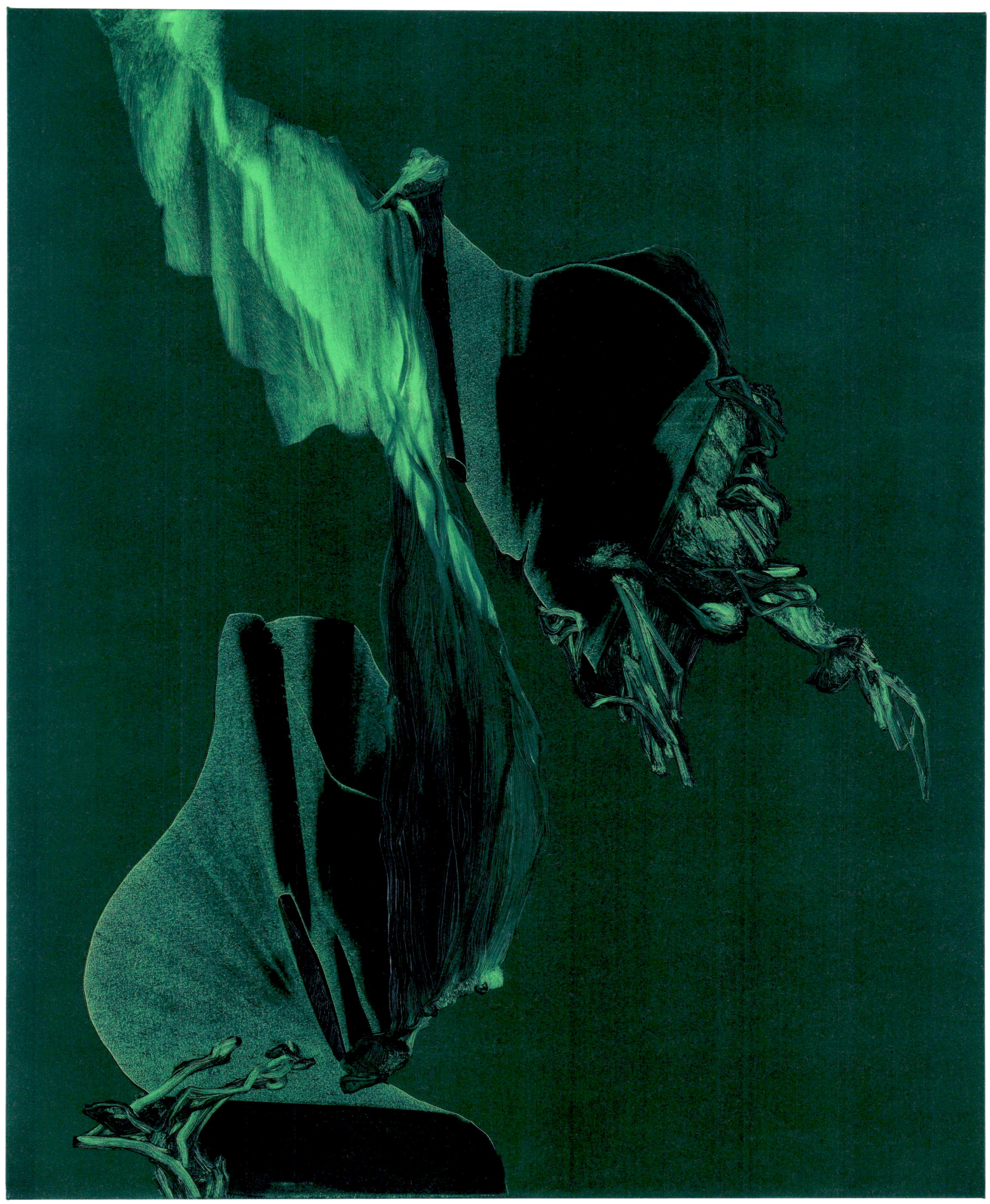

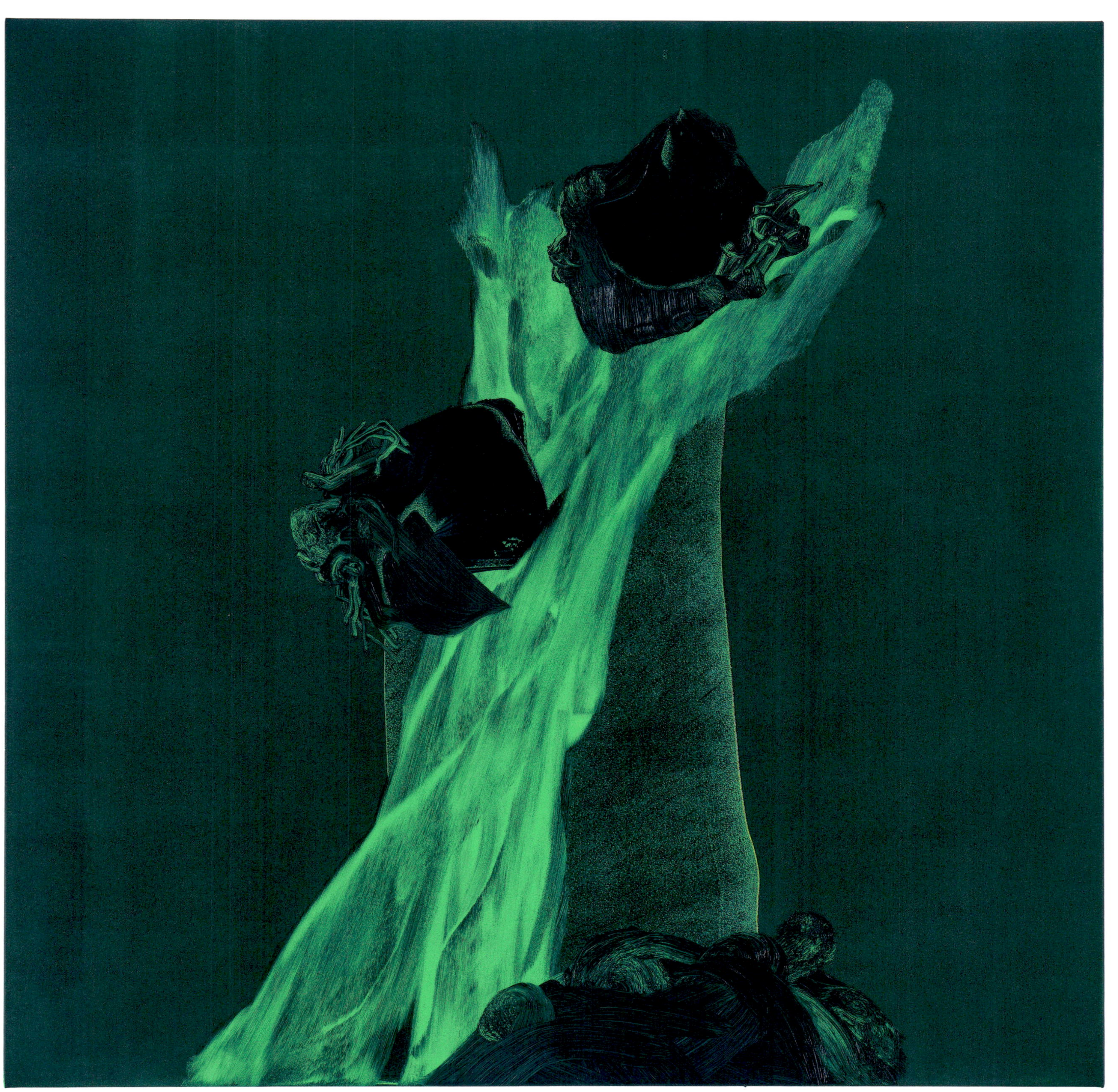

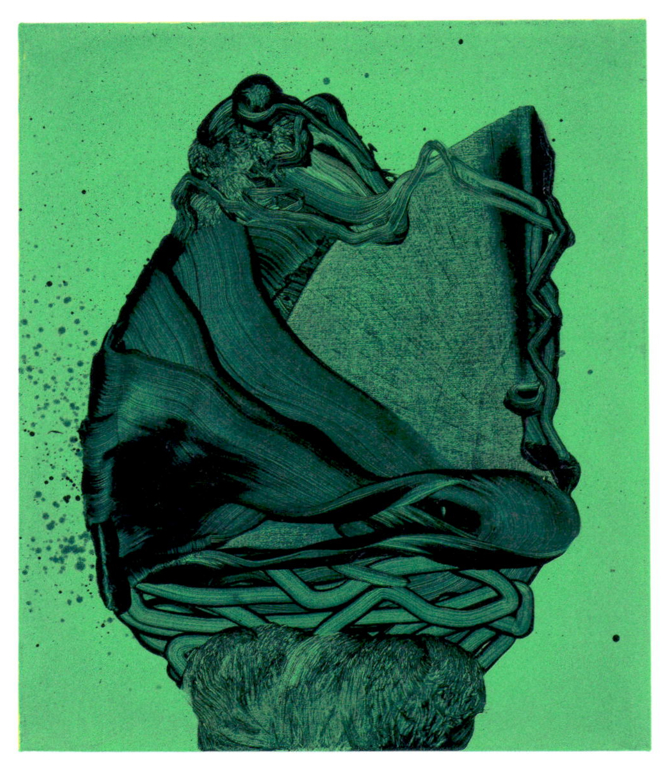

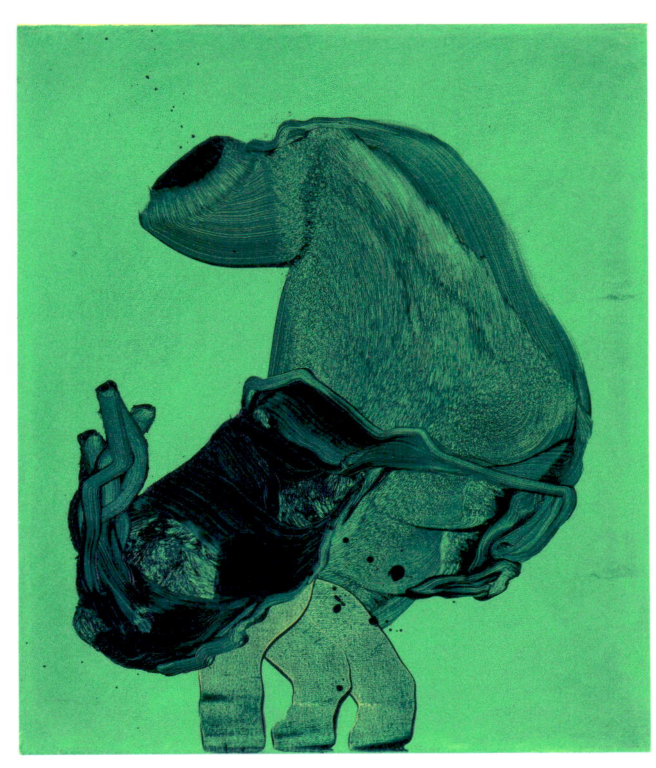

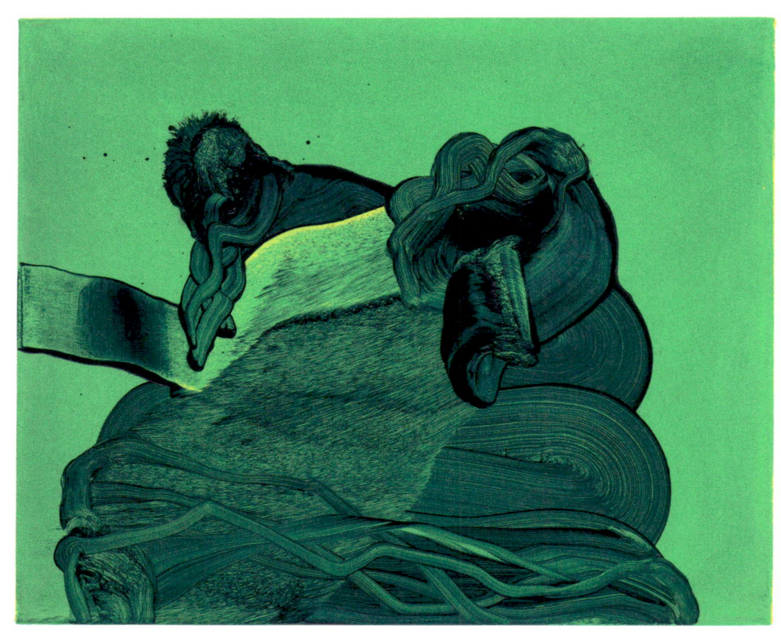

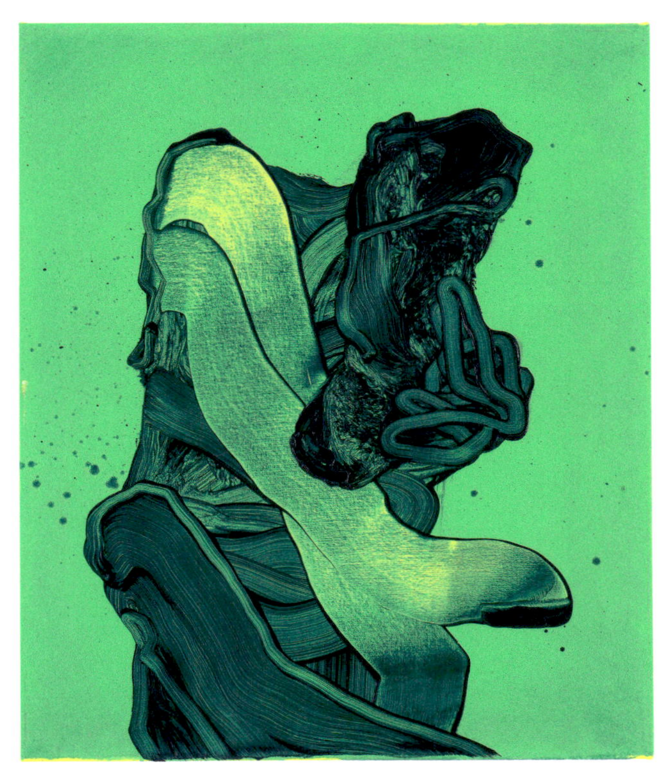

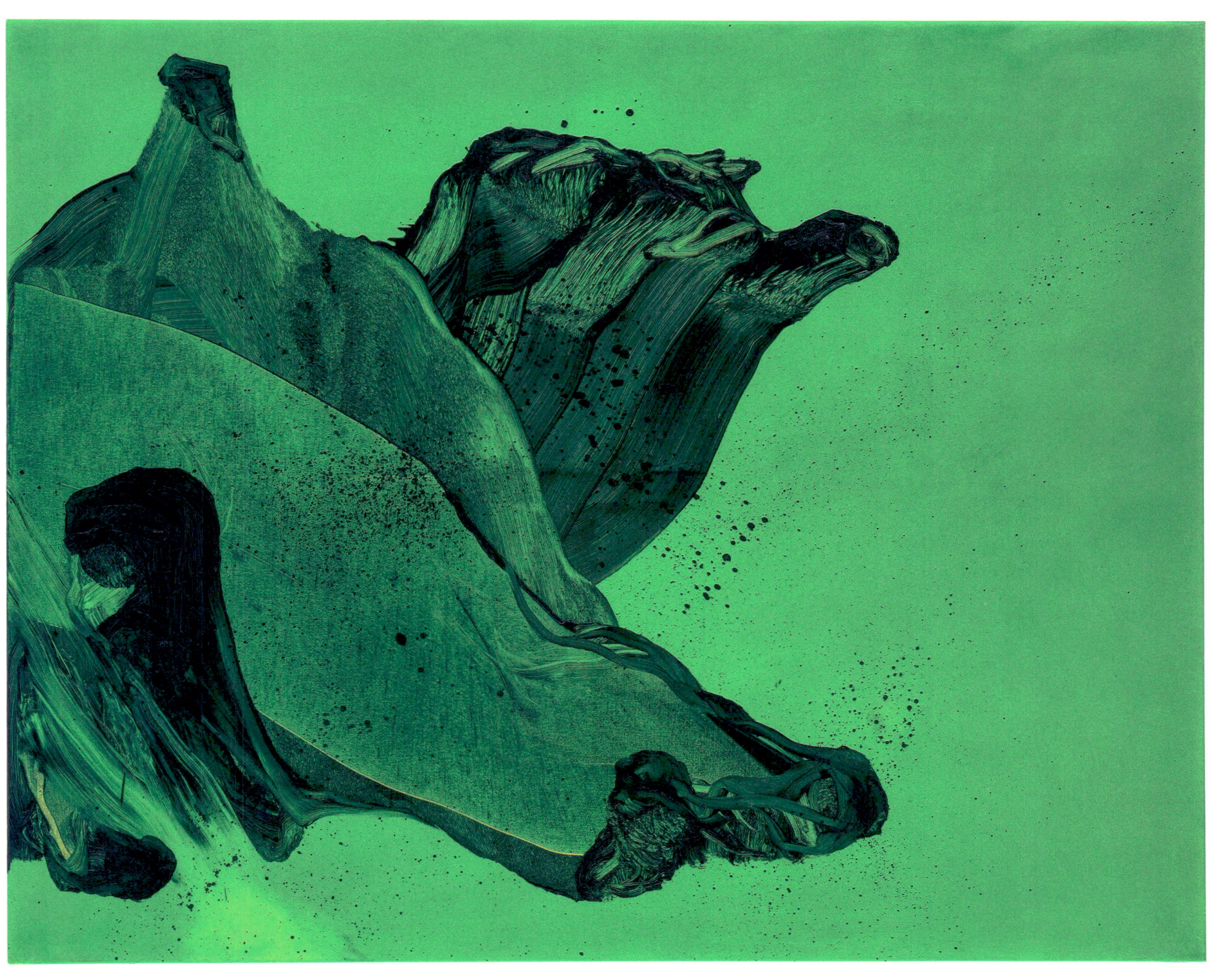

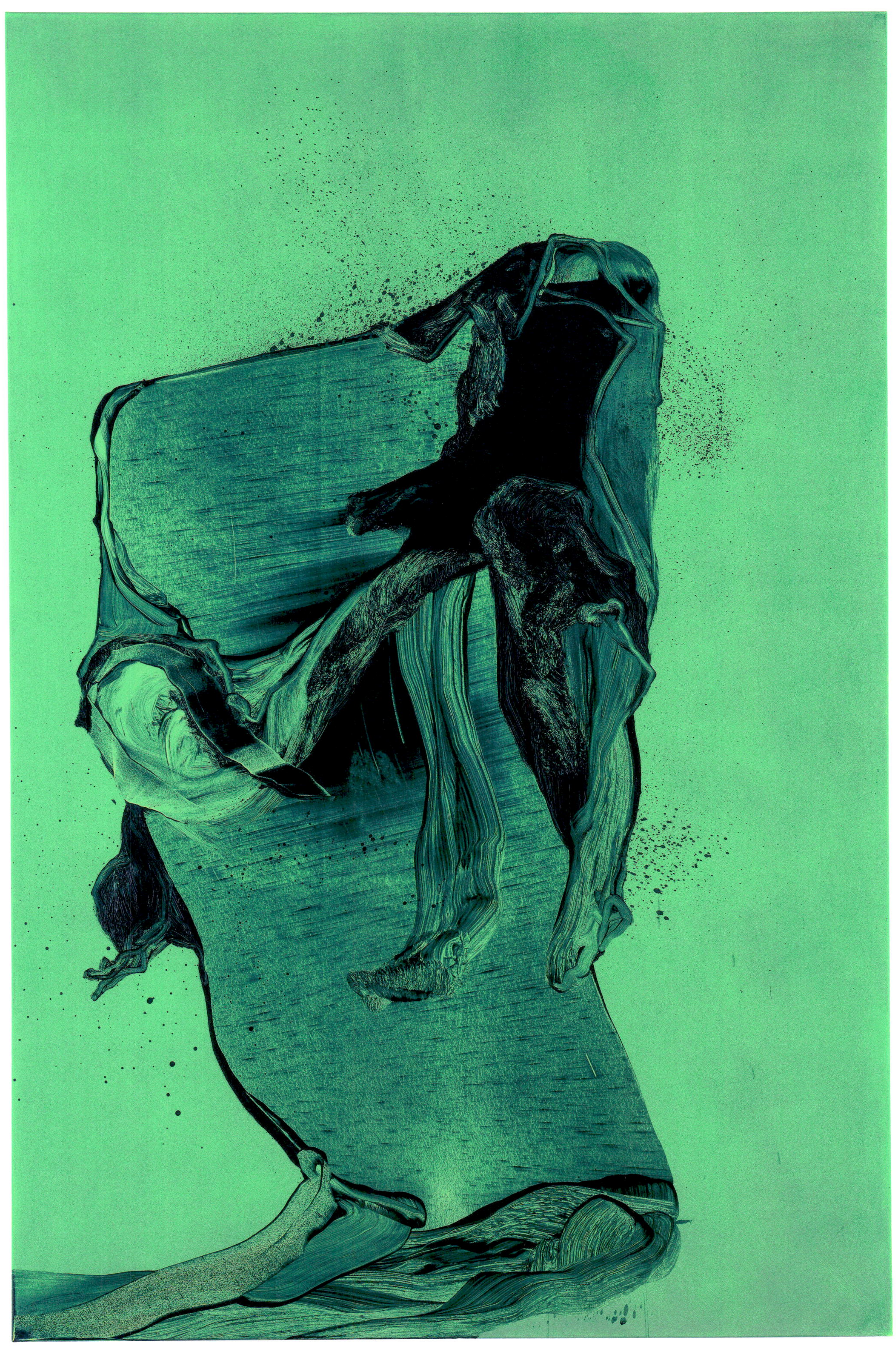

Abbildungsverzeichnis

Herausgeber: Sabine Schmidt, PSM, Berlin

Herstellung: Janine Lattich, Hatje Cantz

Projektmanagement: Juliane Eisele, Hatje Cantz

Lektorat: Sonja Illa-Paschen (Deutsch), Sarah Trenker (Englisch)

Übersetzungen: Elizabeth Volk

Grafische Gestaltung und Satz: Daniel Lergon

Reproduktionen: max-color, Berlin

Fotos: Matthias Kolb (7–17, 21–51, 54, 55, 68, 69, 72–79, 83–91, 94–103, 106–123); Simon Vogel (18, 19); Dinis Santos (52, 53); Roberto Apa (70, 71); Daniel Lergon (81); Kamil Macioł (92, 93); Markus Gröteke / architectureshooting (104, 105)

Druck und Bindung: DZA Druckerei zu Altenburg GmbH, Altenburg

Papier: Gardapat Bianka 150 g/m²

Schrift: Executive Book

Erschienen im
Hatje Cantz Verlag GmbH
Mommsenstraße 27
10629 Berlin
Tel. +49 30 3464678-00
Fax +49 30 3464678-29
www.hatjecantz.de
Ein Unternehmen der Ganske Verlagsgruppe

ISBN 978-3-7757-4513-0

Printed in Germany

Umschlagabbildung:

Detail aus: ohne Titel, 2016, Öl auf Leinwand, 130 × 160 cm

Dank an:
Andersen's Contemporary, Kopenhagen; Åplus, Berlin; Christof und Jochen Beutgen; Dr. Marta Dziomdziora; Galerie Christian Lethert, Köln; Galleria Mario Iannelli, Rom; Marco Gietmann, Berlin; Ivorypress, Madrid; Lena Kiessler; Lazy Mike, Los Angeles/Moskau; Lehmann + Silva, Porto; Dr. Peter Lodermeyer; PSM und Sabine Schmidt, Berlin; Tomasz Switalski; Tomasz Wendland

Privatsammlung, Berlin; Privatsammlung, München; Sammlung Fischer, Rheinbach; Sammlung Iannelli, Rom; Sammlung Heike Klussmann, Berlin; Sammlung Kunstraum am Limes, Hillscheid; Sammlung Frederick Lehmann, Porto; Sammlung Luckey, Lausanne; Sammlung Maier, Zeitkunstgalerie, Kitzbühel; Sammlung Arun Nayar, London; Sammlung Neuhausen, Mönchengladbach; Sammlung Dariusz Wechta, Posen; Sammlung Weikert, Berlin/Schanghai

Tomas Borbás; Mirko Marschewsky; Edwin Mendez; Sara Morcillo; Astrid Rostaing; John Wahlström

Júlia Frate Bolliger; Ursula und Günter Lergon

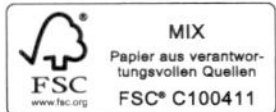